Beyond
Grapes

Simple Recipes for Delicious Homemade Liqueurs

Yacov Morad

LIBRARY TALES PUBLISHING
www.LibraryTalesPublishing.com
www.Facebook.com/LibraryTalesPublishing

For general information on our other products and services, please contact our Customer Care Department at 1-800-754-5016, or fax 917-463-0892. For technical support, please visit
WWW.LIBRARYTALESPUBLISHING.COM

Library Tales Publishing also publishes its books in a variety of electronic formats. Every content that appears in print is available in electronic books.

Edited by Rachel Allen and Kristen Brunelli

*** PRINTED IN THE UNITED STATES OF AMERICA ***

ISBN-13
978-1736241868
978-1736241875

Table of Contents

MIXED LIQUEURS (CONT'D)

STAR ANISE COCONUT LIQUEUR	52	PINEAPPLE ORANGE LIQUEUR	75
GRAPEFRUIT PINEAPPLE LIQUEUR	53	COCONUT GOJI LIQUEUR	76
HONEY LEMON LIQUEUR	54	STRAWBERRY KIWI LIQUEUR	77
CHERRY CINNAMON LIQUEUR	55	PINEAPPLE APPLE LIQUEUR	78
PERFUMED HONEY LIQUEUR	56	APPLE CARDAMOM LIQUEUR	79
BANANA MELON LIQUEUR	57	APPLE MELON LIQUEUR	80
MANGO BANANA LIQUEUR	58	APPLE GINGER LIQUEUR	81
MANGO BLUEBERRY LIQUEUR	59	APPLE DATE LIQUEUR	82
BLACKBERRY BLUEBERRY LIQUEUR	60	MANGO PINEAPPLE LIQUEUR	83
COCONUT PINEAPPLE GINGER	61	NUTS & SESAME LIQUEUR	84
CINNAMON CLOVE LIQUEUR	62	DATE CARDAMOM LIQUEUR	85
COCONUT HONEY LIQUEUR	63	DATE COCOA LIQUEUR	86
COCONUT PINEAPPLE LIQUEUR	64	MELON APRICOT LIQUEUR	87
COCONUT PEACH LIQUEUR	65	COCONUT CINNAMON LIQUEUR	88
PINEAPPLE KIWI LIQUEUR	66	BANANA HONEY LIQUEUR	89
CINNAMON GINGER LIQUEUR	67	PINEAPPLE FIG LIQUEUR	90
COCONUT CHOCOLATE LIQUEUR	68	DATE & NUTS LIQUEUR	91
PLUM RAISIN LIQUEUR	69	CINNAMON DATES LIQUEUR	92
ACAI CAROB LIQUEUR	70	GOJI BERRY PLUM LIQUEUR	93
COCONUT CHERRY LIQUEUR	71	APRICOT BANANA LIQUEUR	94
STRAWBERRY BANANA LIQUEUR	72	MARULA APRICOT LIQUEUR	95
DATE, APPLE CINNAMON LIQUEUR	73	FIG KIWI LIQUEUR	96
STRAWBERRY RAISIN LIQUEUR	74	LEMON MINT LIQUEUR	97
		CHAMOMILE ELDERBERRY LIQUEUR	98

VEGGIE & HERBAL LIQUEURS

LAVENDER LIQUEUR	102	TOMATO LIQUEUR	108
LEMONGRASS LIQUEUR	103	CARROT LIQUEUR	109
SAGE LIQUEUR	104	ARTICHOKE LIQUEUR	110
INDIAN ROSE LIQUEUR	105	KOHLRABI LIQUEUR	111
MINT DILL LIQUEUR	106	BEET LIQUEUR	112
BRUSSELS SPROUTS LIQUEUR	107	FENNEL LIQUEUR	113

HOMEMADE VODKA

STAR ANISE VODKA	116	COCONUT VODKA	118
PINEAPPLE VODKA	117	APPLE VODKA	119
		CINNAMON VODKA	120

HOMEMADE MOONSHINE

POMEGRANATE DELIGHT	124	APPLE SEASON	126
PLUMS FOR DAYS	125		

Foreword

My name is Yacov Morad. I am the founder of the world-famous Morad Winery in Israel. Over the past fifty-five years, I've been happily married to my wife Ester, with whom I've helped raise four beautiful sons, two grandsons, and two granddaughters. Not only have I been blessed with a wonderful family, but I have also been able to provide for them doing the thing I love most: making wines and liqueurs out of anything BUT grapes.

When I was about ten years old, I saw my father picking grapes in the family vineyard, squeezing them in reverence, dropping them in clay jugs, and preparing them for fermentation. Even then I remember being hypnotized by the smell of fermentation and the aroma of freshly squeezed grapes. This is when I fell in love with wine, so much in fact that by the tender age of twelve I was already making wine on my own. In 1968, I met my future wife Ester. I told her all about my passion for winemaking, and she informed me that her father also made wines, but that his were of a particular variety. One day, I was invited to Ester's house. Following "cordial guest" norms, I decided to bring with me a bottle of homemade wine. I gave her father the bottle, and then he looked at me and said, "Let me show you my wine." He handed me a strangely colored glass of wine; it was delicious! The flavor was one that I had never tasted before. I asked him what it was, and he replied with a smile, "Pumpkin wine!"

Ester's father opened my eyes to a new type of wine, one that can be made from anything and everything. From pomegranates to apples and carrots, the flavors were mesmerizing, and their taste captured my heart and created a spark in my imagination. After getting married, my wife and I moved to a small village in Northern Israel, and in the basement of our tiny home were all sorts of bottles containing fermented wines and liqueurs from fruits, vegetables, and medicinal plants.

For thirty-five years I developed countless types of wines and liqueurs in the comfort of my own home until I finally decided to turn my life-long hobby into a full-time business and open my very own winery. Morad Winery received a surprising amount of publicity in radio, television, and the press, primarily because of the uniqueness of the wines and liqueurs that were made there. The winery has been visited by thousands of tourists, celebrities, and influential figures in the world of wine, from Israel and abroad. Having so many people visit and appreciate my love of unique wines and liqueurs has given me so much pride in my life, and now I can share my love and knowledge with you, through these series of books.

The first "Beyond Grapes" book was created as a fun wine recipe book that exposed wine enthusiasts to a new way of making wine. Within the body of the work were some liqueur recipes as well. Now, by popular demand, I decided to create a second book, one that focuses primarily on making delicious, mouthwatering liqueurs from any fruit, vegetable, or medicinal herb you can imagine.

Yacov Morad

A BRIEF OVERVIEW OF THE
LIQUEUR MAKING PROCESS

The first step in the process of making any one of the specialty recipes included in this book is to gather together all the things you will need. This includes all the containers, lids, and other utensils, appliances, and tools required, as well as the general ingredients for liqueur-making.

All the necessary utensils and tools can be bought at any store that sells wine-making equipment, or you can find them online.

(1) TWO HERMETIC JARS
These hermetic jars must be suitable for food use. They can be made of glass, plastic, or metal. Each jar must be large enough to hold at least 1 liter of liquid.

(2) A LARGE POT
Any large cooking pot would do.

(3) TWO EMPTY, CLEAN BOTTLES
(4) A STRAINER OR CHEESECLOTH
(5) A FUNNEL
(6) A MEASURING CUP
(7) TUPPERWARE OR A CONTAINER FOR FRUIT LEFTOVERS

MAKING LIQUEURS

(1) To begin each and every recipe you must put a fruit, herb, or medicinal plant into a hermetic glass jar. I prefer using dry fruit because it's available year-round and makes less of a mess in the kitchen.

(2) Next, you must add vodka or alcohol and seal hermetically. "Hermetically" means to seal air-tight to protect your liquor from bacteria.

(3) Over the course of a few days, or weeks, depending on the recipe, the alcohol will absorb the taste, smell, and color of the fruit. The fruit will also absorb some of the alcohol as well. This process is called "extraction." The amount of time it takes to fully extract flavors will vary on the base you use, whether it be fruit, vegetable, or medicinal herb.

(4) Once extraction is complete, strain the extract into a new jar and seal tightly.

(5) Create a simple syrup by dissolving the sugar in simmering water on a low heat, consistently stirring until the sugar is dissolved.

(6) Let your simple syrup cool, then combine with the extract. You have now made your brew.

(7) Seal the brew and allow the liqueur to age. Each recipe's aging time is different. Aging is important because it allows the flavors to settle. The longer the liqueur ages, the better it will taste.

(7) Once the aging process is complete, you can enjoy your home-made liqueur.

SOME NOTES, THOUGHTS, AND IDEAS

<u>Sugar Alternatives</u>
If you are looking for a sugar alternative in these recipes, we recommend using an erythritol sweetener. Erythritol is a tasteless, healthy sweetener that's about 70% less sweet than cane sugar. You could substitute sugar for erythritol using a 1/1 ratio. Instead of 100 grams of sugar, use 100 grams of erythritol. Erythritol dissolves very quickly in water, especially in hot water, making it the perfect sugar substitute.

A – You could and should eat the alcohol-soaked fruits! Since we use dry fruits, they don't disintegrate during the extraction process. So, you end up with a delicious, alcohol-soaked fruit. You could serve these over a cake or dessert, blended in a smoothie, in a fruit salad, or just eat them plain.

* Please eat responsibly :)

B – At the end of the process, a sediment is formed at the bottom of the bottle. You could filter that out using a cheesecloth, or simply drink it along with your liqueur. After all, it's still fruit.

C – Once the extraction is complete, make sure you taste the brew. If it's too sweet, add vodka. If it's not sweet enough, add sugar or erythritol.

D – Shake the bottle well before serving. Serve cold for best results.

Specialty Liqueurs

ADD A NUTELLA LIQUEUR TO
YOUR FAVORITE CHOCOLATE
MILKSHAKE RECIPE.
SPRUCE IT UP WITH
COOKIES AND CREAM.

Chestnut Liqueur

Ingredients
(for making 1 Liter, 18.5% alcohol)

- 480ml Vodka
- 450ml Water
- 250g Chopped Chestnuts
- 160g Sugar
- 6ml Organic Vanilla Extract

> **1 Liter = 0.264 Gallon**
> **1 Gram = 0.035 Ounces**
> **1 ml = 0.033 oz**

The Process

(1) Combine chopped chestnuts and vodka into a glass jar and seal hermetically for 14 days.

(2) Once the 14 days have passed, filter the chestnut extract into a new jar and discard the leftover chestnuts.

(3) Bring water to a simmer and add the sugar and vanilla. Stir until the sugar has dissolved, cover and let cool.

(4) Add the simple syrup to the chestnut extract and mix well.

(5) Pour the final chestnut brew into a bottle, and seal for 14 days.

(6) Shake before serving. Serve cold.

Mushroom Liqueur

Ingredients
(for making 1 Liter, 18% alcohol)

- 470ml Vodka
- 470ml Water
- 2ml Organic Vanilla Extract
- 170g Sugar
- 60g Dried Mitaki Mushrooms
- 24g Dried Shiitake Mushrooms
- 2g Moringa Leaves

The Process

(1) Combine the mushrooms, moringa leaves, and vodka into a clean, sanitized glass jar and seal hermetically for 14 days.

(2) Once the 14 days have passed, strain the extract into a new jar and seal tightly. Discard the leftover mushrooms.

(3) Bring water to a simmer and add the sugar and vanilla. Stir until the sugar has dissolved, cover, and let cool.

(4) Add the simple syrup to the mushroom extract and mix well.

(5) Pour the final brew into a bottle, and seal hermetically for 14 days.

(6) Shake before serving. Serve cold.

Pistachio Liqueur

Ingredients
(for making 1 Liter, 18% alcohol)

• 450ml Vodka
• 450ml Water
• 4ml Organic Vanilla Extract
• 160g Sugar
• 100g Pistachios

The Process

(1) Chop the pistachios and place in a clean, sanitized glass jar, add the vodka and seal hermetically for 14 days.

(2) Once the 14 days have passed, strain the extract into a new jar and seal tightly.

(3) Bring water to a simmer and add the sugar and vanilla. Stir until dissolved, then cover and let cool.

(4) Add the simple syrup to the brew and mix well.

(5) Pour the final brew into a bottle, and seal hermetically for 14 days.

(6) Shake before serving. Serve cold.

Sambuca

Ingredients
(for making 1 Liter, 20% alcohol)

- 500ml Vodka
- 400ml Water
- 4ml Organic Vanilla Extract
- 160g Sugar
- 30g Chopped Hazelnuts
- 6g Star Anise
- 6g Black Elderberries
- 5g Crushed Coffee Beans

The Process

(1) In a clean, sanitized glass jar combine the star anise, crushed coffee beans, black elderberries, chopped hazelnuts, and vodka. Seal hermetically and leave in a cool, dark place for 14 days.

(2) Once the 14 days have passed, strain the extract into a clean glass bottle and seal.

(3) In a metal pot, combine the sugar and water and stir on a low simmer. Stir until the sugar is dissolved, then add the vanilla extract and allow to cool.

(4) Once the syrup has cooled, combine the spice extract with the syrup and stir again to combine.

(5) Pour into a clean bottle and seal. Store this for another 14 days.

(6) Shake before serving. Serve cold.

Nutella Liqueur

Ingredients
(for making 1 Liter, 18% alcohol)

• 500ml Vodka
• 190ml Water
• 120ml Almond Milk
• 80ml Coconut Water
• 4ml Organic Vanilla Extract
• 180g Nutella Spread
• 160g Sugar
• 5g Cocoa Powder

The Process

(1) Combine sugar and cocoa powder into a pot and stir to combine.

(2) In a separate pot, boil water. Add the cocoa powder and sugar while stirring continuously. Once the sugar has dissolved, add the Nutella and stir on a low heat until evenly incorporated.

(3) Once this is a smooth and creamy consistency, add the coconut water and almond milk and stir to combine.

(4) Remove from the heat and stir in the vanilla. Cover this for an hour so the flavors have time to blend together.

(5) Once the mixture has cooled, slowly add vodka while stirring to evenly incorporate. Once it's thoroughly mixed, pour into a clean bottle and seal for 14 days.

(6) Shake well before serving. Serve cold.

Instant Chocolate Liqueur

Ingredients
(for making 1 Liter, 17.5% alcohol)

- 380ml Vodka
- 480ml Water
- 5ml Organic Vanilla Extract
- 230g Sugar
- 100g Hot Chocolate Powder
- 30g Dark Cocoa Powder

The Process

(1) Combine sugar, cocoa powder, and instant hot chocolate powder inside a large pot and mix all the ingredients together.

(2) In another pot, boil the water, pour the mixtured powder, and stir to combine while adding the vanilla extract. Cover and place to the side to cool.

(3) After cooling, add vodka and stir until you have a smooth and creamy texture.

(4) Pour into a bottle and seal for 14 days.

(5) Shake well before serving. Serve cold.

Cola Liqueur

Ingredients
(for making 1 Liter, 20% alcohol)

- 530ml Vodka
- 400ml Coca-Cola
- 4ml Organic Vanilla Extract
- 180g Sugar
- 15g Cinnamon Sticks
- 15g Crushed Coffee Beans
- 15g Kola Nut

The Process

(1) Combine in a clean, sanitized glass jar the cinnamon sticks, coffee beans, kola nuts, and vodka, and seal hermetically for 15 days.

(2) Once the 15 days have passed, strain the extract into a bottle and close. Discard the remaining ingredients.

(3) Pour the Coca-Cola into a pot, combine with sugar and vanilla, and continuously stir on a low simmer until the sugar dissolves.

(4) Once this mixture has cooled, add the cinnamon-nut extract from the bottle and stir well.

(5) Strain and transfer the final mixture into a bottle and store in a cool, dark place for 20 days.

(6) Shake before serving. Serve cold.

Hazelnut Liqueur

Ingredients
(for making 1 Liter, 18% alcohol)

- 460ml Vodka
- 440ml Water
- 4ml Organic Vanilla Extract
- 180g Sugar
- 150g Hazelnuts

The Process

(1) In a clean, sanitized glass jar add the vodka and hazelnuts, seal hermetically. Store in a cool, dark place for 15 days.

(2) Once the 15 days have passed, strain the liquid from the brew into a bottle and seal. Discard the leftover hazelnuts.

(3) Next, add the sugar and water into a pot and simmer while continuously stirring until the sugar is dissolved. Once the sugar is dissolved, add the vanilla extract. Remove from heat and allow the mixture to cool.

(4) Once the simple syrup is cooled, add the hazelnut extract from the bottle and stir to combine.

(5) Pour the final hazelnut mixture into a clean bottle and seal for 14 days.

(6) Shake well before serving. Serve cold.

Halvah Liqueur

Ingredients
(for making 1 Liter, 17% alcohol)

- 430ml Vodka
- 400ml Water
- 4ml Organic Vanilla Extract
- 180g Sugar
- 130g Halvah

The Process

(1) In a clean metal pot combine the water and the sugar and stir on a simmer until the sugar is dissolved.

(2) Once the sugar is dissolved, add the halvah and stir until it is dissolved. Once the halvah is dissolved, add the vanilla extract. Remove from heat and allow the simple syrup to cool.

(3) Next, add the vodka to the cooled halvah syrup and pour into a hermetically sealed bottle. Store in a cool, dark place for 14 days.

(4) Shake well before serving. Serve cold.

Peanut Butter Liqueur

Ingredients
(for making 1 Liter, 18% alcohol)

- 500ml Vodka
- 200ml Water
- 120ml Coconut Water
- 4ml Organic Vanilla Extract
- 200g Peanut Butter (Creamy)
- 160g Sugar
- 4g Dark Cocoa Powder

The Process

(1) In a large, clean pot add the peanut butter, sugar, cocoa powder and stir on low heat. Once the peanut butter mixture is smooth and evenly incorporated, add the coconut water.

(2) After the coconut water is evenly incorporated into the peanut butter mixture, turn the heat off and add the vanilla extract. Remove from heat to let cool so flavors blend together.

(3) Next, slowly add the vodka to the peanut butter mixture and stir until it is evenly incorporated.

(4) Once the mixture is thoroughly mixed together, pour it into a clean bottle and seal. Place in a cool, dark place for 14 days.

(5) Shake before serving. Serve cold.

Fruit Liqueurs

BANANA COCKTAIL, SERVED
WITH FRESH PASSION FRUIT AND
GARNISHED WITH FRUIT PEELS.

Plum Liqueur

Ingredients
(for making 1 Liter, 20% alcohol)

- 300ml Vodka
- 200ml Water
- 3ml Organic Vanilla Extract
- 280g Ripe Plums
- 120g Sugar

The Process

(1) In a clean, sanitized glass jar, add the plum fruit and vodka.

(2) Seal tightly and place in a cool, dark place for 10 days.

(3) Once the 10 days have passed, strain the fruit and pour the liquid into a bottle and seal. Feel free to eat the leftover fruit.

(4) Combine the sugar and water in a pot and stir on a low simmer until the sugar dissolves.

(5) Stir the vanilla extract into the simple syrup and allow to cool.

(6) Once the vanilla simple syrup has cooled, stir in the fermented plum mixture. Pour this final mixture into a bottle and store in a cool, dark place for 10 days.

(7) Shake well before serving. Serve cold.

Grapefruit Liqueur

Ingredients
(for making 1 Liter, 19% alcohol)

• 500ml Vodka
• 400ml Water
• 120g Red Grapefruit Slices
• 160g Sugar

The Process

(1) In a clean, sanitized glass jar add the vodka and grapefruit slices. Seal hermetically and store in a cool, dark place for 10 days.

(2) Once the 10 days have passed, strain the liquid into a bowl. Do not squeeze the remaining fruit as it will make the mixture bitter. Pour the remaining liquid into a bottle, and seal.

(3) Next, add the sugar and water into a pot and simmer while continuously stirring until the sugar is dissolved.

(4) Once the simple syrup has dissolved, remove from heat and let cool before adding the grapefruit extract.

(5) Pour the final mixture into a clean bottle and seal for 10 days.

(6) Shake well before serving. Serve cold.

Prickly Pear Liqueur

Ingredients
(for making 1 Liter, 21% alcohol)

- 540ml Vodka
- 350ml Water
- 180g Sugar
- 400g Ripe Prickly Pear, Peeled

The Process

(1) Clean and slice peeled prickly pears into circular disks and place in a clean glass jar. Then add vodka and seal hermetically in a cool, dark place for 10 days.

(2) Once the 10 days have passed, place a clean cheesecloth in a bowl and pour the prickly pear mixture into it. Then squeeze the cheesecloth in order to extract as much liquid as possible.

(3) Pour the extract into a bottle and seal. You can discard the leftover fruit or eat it as an adult treat.

(4) Next, combine the sugar and water in a metal pot and simmer while stirring until the sugar has dissolved.

(5) Allow the simple syrup to cool before adding the fruit extract you made 10 days before. Stir well before pouring into a bottle and sealing for an additional 10 days.

(6) Shake well before serving. Serve cold.

Grape Liqueur

Ingredients
(for making 1 Liter, 18% alcohol)

- 460ml Vodka
- 400ml Water
- 250g Sugar
- 400g Dark Grapes
- 200g Dark Raisins

The Process

(1) In a clean, sanitized glass jar, combine the grapes, raisins, and vodka. Seal hermetically and store in a cool, dark place for 10 days.

(2) Once the 10 days have passed, strain the extract into a clean glass jar and seal hermetically.

(3) In a metal pot, simmer the sugar and water and stir until the sugar is dissolved.

(4) After the simple syrup has cooled, add the extract from the bottle to the simple syrup and stir well.

(5) Pour the combined mixture into a bottle and store for 10 days.

(6) Shake well before serving. Serve cold.

Peach Liqueur

Ingredients
(for making 1 Liter, 20% alcohol)

- 520ml Vodka
- 360ml Water
- 200g Sugar
- 250g Dried Peach
- 100g Light Raisins

The Process

(1) Add the dried peach, raisins, and vodka into glass jar, and seal hermetically for 10 days in a cool, dark place.

(2) Once the 10 days have passed, strain the extract into a clean hermetic jar and seal. Feel free to eat the leftover fruit as an adult snack.

(3) In a metal pot, combine the sugar and water and stir on a low simmer. Stir until the sugar is dissolved, allow to cool.

(4) Once the simple syrup has cooled, add the extract and stir to combine.

(5) Pour the final brew into a bottle, and seal for 10 days.

(6) Shake before serving. Serve cold.

Apple Cider Liqueur

Ingredients
(for making 1 Liter, 18% alcohol)

• 480ml Vodka
• 460ml Apple Juice
• 2ml Organic Vanilla Extract
• 180g Sugar
• 25g Broken Cinnamon Sticks
• 0.6g Whole Cloves

The Process

(1) Put the cloves in a clean, sanitized jar, then add the broken cinnamon sticks and vodka. Seal hermetically and leave in a dark and cool place for 14 days.

(2) Once the 14 days have passed, strain the extract into a glass bottle and seal.

(3) Next, pour apple juice into a metal pot and simmer on a low setting. Once the apple juice is simmering, add the sugar and stir until it dissolves.

(4) Add your vanilla extract to the apple simple syrup and stir to combine. Turn the heat off and allow the mixture to cool.

(5) Pour your cooled mixture into bottles and seal tightly for another 14 days.

(6) Shake before serving. Serve cold.

Blueberry Liqueur

Ingredients
(for making 1 Liter, 19% alcohol)

- 490ml Vodka
- 200ml Water
- 4ml Organic Vanilla Extract
- 160g Blueberries
- 140g Sugar
- 50g Light Honey

The Process

(1) In a clean, sanitized glass jar add the vodka and blueberries and seal hermetically. Store in a cool, dark place for 10 days.

(2) Once the 10 days have passed, strain the liquid from the brew into a bottle and seal. You can either discard the blueberries or blend them up with some ice for a delicious adult smoothie.

(3) Next, add the honey, sugar, and water into a pot and simmer (do not boil) while continuously stirring until the sugar is dissolved.

(4) Once the simple syrup is cooled, add the vanilla extract and blueberry extract from the bottle and stir to combine.

(5) Pour the final blueberry mixture into a clean bottle and seal for 7 days.

(6) Shake well before serving. Serve cold.

Persimmon Liqueur

Ingredients
(for making 1 Liter, 19% alcohol)

- 480ml Vodka
- 400ml Water
- 360g Ripe Persimmon
- 200g Sugar

The Process

(1) In a clean, sanitized glass jar add the vodka and persimmon and seal hermetically. Store in a cool, dark place for 10 days.

(2) Once the 10 days have passed, gently strain the persimmon extract into a bottle and seal.

(3) Next, combine the sugar and water into a pot and simmer while continuously stirring until the sugar is dissolved. Take the simple syrup off the stove and let cool.

(4) Add the persimmon extract to the simple syrup and mix again. Pour the mixture into a bottle and store in a cool place for 10 days.

(5) Shake well before serving. Serve cold.

Banana Liqueur

Ingredients
(for making 1 Liter, 18.5% alcohol)

- 500ml Vodka
- 400ml Water
- 400g Ripe Banana Peels
- 180g Sugar

The Process

(1) In a clean, sanitized glass jar add the vodka and banana peels and seal hermetically. Store in a cool, dark place for 10 days.

(2) Once the 10 days have passed, gently strain the liquid from the brew into a bottle and seal. Discard the leftover peels.

(3) Next, add the sugar and water into a pot and simmer while continuously stirring until the sugar is dissolved. Remove from heat and let cool.

(4) Once the simple syrup is cooled, add the banana extract from the bottle and stir to combine.

(5) Pour the final banana mixture into a clean bottle and seal for 10 days.

(6) Shake well before serving. Serve cold.

Maple Liqueur

Ingredients
(for making 1 Liter, 18% alcohol)

- 460ml Vodka
- 240ml Organic Maple Syrup
- 220ml Water
- 2ml Organic Vanilla Extract
- 130g Sugar

The Process

(1) Combine the sugar and water into a pot and simmer while continuously stirring until the sugar is dissolved.

(2) Once the sugar is dissolved, add the maple syrup, cover, and allow to cool.

(3) Once the maple simple syrup is cooled, add the vodka, and stir to combine.

(4) Pour the final maple mixture into a clean bottle and seal for 10 days.

(5) Shake before serving. Serve cold.

Mixed Liqueurs

PIÑA COLADA, MIXED WITH
PINEAPPLE APRICOT LIQUEUR

Citrus
Celebration

Ingredients

(for making 1 Liter, 21% alcohol)

- 550ml Vodka
- 130ml Orange Juice
- 200ml Water
- 230g Sugar
- 120g Whole Kumquats
- 100g Lemon Peels
- 80g Mandarin Peels

The Process

(1) In a clean, sanitized glass jar add the vodka, kumquats, lemon peels, and mandarin peels. Seal tightly and place in a dark and cool place for 15 days.

(2) Once the 15 days have passed, strain the liquid into a bowl. Do not squeeze the remaining fruit as it will make the mixture bitter. Pour the remaining liquid into a bottle, and seal.

(3) Next, add the sugar and water into a pot and simmer while continuously stirring until the sugar is dissolved. Add the orange juice and allow the mixture to cool.

(4) Once the orange simple syrup has cooled to room temperature, add the kumquat extract and stir well.

(5) Pour into a clean bottle and seal for 10 days.

(6) Shake well before serving. Serve cold.

Pineapple Apricot Liqueur

Ingredients
(for making 1 Liter, 20% alcohol)

- 500ml Vodka
- 380ml Water
- 190g Sugar
- 120g Dried Pineapple
- 80g Dried Apricot
- 40g Light Raisins

The Process

(1) In a clean, sanitized glass jar add the vodka, pineapple, apricot, and raisins and seal hermetically. Store in a cool, dark place for 10 days.

(2) Once the 10 days have passed, strain the liquid from the brew into a bottle and seal. Feel free to eat the remaining fruit as an adult snack.

(3) Next, add the sugar and water into a pot and simmer while continuously stirring until the sugar is dissolved. Remove from heat and allow the simple syrup to cool.

(4) Once the simple syrup is cooled, add the pineapple extract from the bottle and stir to combine.

(5) Transfer the final mixture into a clean bottle and seal for 10 days.

(6) Shake well before serving. Serve cold.

Apple Coconut Liqueur

Ingredients

(for making 1 Liter, 18% alcohol)

- 480ml Vodka
- 440ml Water
- 180g Sugar
- 100g Dried Apple
- 80g Coconut Chips
- 20g Light Raisins

The Process

(1) In a clean, sanitized glass jar add the vodka, apple, coconut chips, and raisins and seal hermetically. Store in a cool, dark place for 14 days.

(2) Once the 14 days have passed, strain the liquid from the brew into a bottle and seal. Feel free to eat the remaining fruit as an adult snack.

(3) Next, add the sugar and water into a pot and simmer while continuously stirring until the sugar is dissolved. Remove from heat and allow the mixture to cool.

(4) Once the simple syrup is cooled, add the coconut and apple extract from the bottle and stir to combine.

(5) Pour the coconut and apple extract into a clean bottle and seal for 14 days.

(6) Shake well before serving. Serve cold.

Goji Berry Pineapple Liqueur

Ingredients
(for making 1 Liter, 20% alcohol)

• 520ml Vodka
• 380ml Water
• 180g Sugar
• 100g Goji Berry
• 100g Dried Pineapple
• 40g Light Raisins

The Process

(1) In a clean, sanitized glass jar add the vodka, goji berry, pineapple, and raisins and seal hermetically. Store in a cool, dark place for 10 days.

(2) Once the 10 days have passed, strain the liquid from the brew into a bottle and seal. Feel free to eat the remaining fruit as an adult snack.

(3) Next, add the sugar and water into a pot and simmer while continuously stirring until the sugar is dissolved. Remove from heat and allow the simple syrup to cool.

(4) Once the simple syrup is cooled, add the goji berry extract from the bottle and stir to combine.

(5) Transfer the final mixture into a clean bottle and seal for 10 days.

(6) Shake well before serving. Serve cold.

Carob & Honey Liqueur

Ingredients

(for making 1 Liter, 20% alcohol)

• 510ml Vodka
• 300ml Water
• 4ml Organic Vanilla Extract
• 100g Carob Honey
• 120g Light Honey
• 40g Sugar

The Process

(1) In a clean metal pot simmer the water, sugar, carob honey, and light honey on low heat and stir until dissolved.

(2) Remove the honey simple syrup from heat and add the vanilla extract. Cover and let cool for at least one hour to allow the flavors to blend together.

(3) Once cooled, add the vodka and pour the final mixture into a bottle. Seal hermetically for 10 days.

(4) Shake well before serving. Serve cold.

Mango Date Liqueur

Ingredients

(for making 1 Liter, 20% alcohol)

- 500ml Vodka
- 350ml Water
- 4ml Organic Vanilla Extract
- 120g Dried Mango
- 100g Sugar
- 80g Dates
- 30g Black Raisins

The Process

(1) In a clean, sanitized glass jar add the vodka, mango, dates, and raisins and seal hermetically. Store in a cool, dark place for 10 days.

(2) Once the 10 days have passed, strain the liquid from the brew into a bottle and seal. Feel free to eat the remaining fruit as an adult snack.

(3) Next, add the sugar and water into a pot and simmer while continuously stirring until the sugar is dissolved. Remove from heat and allow the mixture to cool.

(4) Once the simple syrup is cooled, add the vanilla extract and mango-date extract from the bottle and stir to combine.

(5) Pour the final mango-date extract into a clean bottle and seal for 7 days.

(6) Shake well before serving. Serve cold.

Fig & Nut Liqueur

Ingredients

(for making 1 Liter, 20% alcohol)

• 520ml Vodka
• 400ml Water
• 4ml Organic Vanilla Extract
• 150g Dried Figs
• 150g Sugar
• 60g Walnuts
• 60g Pecans

The Process

(1) In a clean, sanitized glass jar add the vodka, figs, walnuts, and pecans and seal hermetically. Store in a cool, dark place for 15 days.

(2) Once the 15 days have passed, strain the liquid from the brew into a bottle and seal. Feel free to eat the remaining fruit as an adult snack but discard the nuts.

(3) Next, add the sugar and water into a pot and simmer while continuously stirring until the sugar is dissolved. Remove from heat and allow to cool.

(4) Once the simple syrup is cooled, add the vanilla extract and fig-nut extract from the bottle and stir to combine.

(5) Pour the final fig-nut extract into a clean bottle and seal for 14 days.

(6) Shake well before serving. Serve cold.

Coconut & Coffee Liqueur

Ingredients
(for making 1 Liter, 18% alcohol)

- 480ml Vodka
- 400ml Water
- 4ml Organic Vanilla Extract
- 120g Coconut Chips
- 200g Sugar
- 20g Instant Coffee

The Process

(1) In a clean, sanitized glass jar add the coconut chips to vodka and seal hermetically. Store in a cool, dark place for 15 days.

(2) Once the 15 days have passed, strain the liquid from the brew into a bottle and seal.

(3) Next, add the sugar, instant coffee, and water into a pot and simmer while continuously stirring until the sugar and coffee had dissolved. Add the vanilla extract, cover, and allow to cool for 30 minutes.

(4) Once the simple syrup is cooled, combine with the brew and stir well.

(5) Pour the final brew into a clean bottle and seal for 14 days.

(6) Shake well before serving. Serve cold.

Mango & Apple Liqueur

Ingredients

(for making 1 Liter, 20% alcohol)

• 520ml Vodka
• 430ml Water
• 140g Sugar
• 80g Dried Mango
• 80g Dried Apple
• 60g Light Raisins

The Process

(1) In a clean, sanitized glass jar add the vodka, mango, apple, and raisins and seal hermetically. Store in a cool, dark place for 10 days.

(2) Once the 10 days have passed, strain the liquid from the brew into a bottle and seal.

(3) Next, add the sugar and water into a pot and simmer while continuously stirring until the sugar is dissolved. Remove from heat and allow the mixture to cool.

(4) Once the simple syrup is cooled, add the mango-apple extract from the bottle and stir to combine.

(5) Pour the final mango-apple mixture into a clean bottle and seal for 10 days.

(6) Shake well before serving. Serve cold.

Acai & Plum Liqueur

Ingredients
(for making 1 Liter, 19% alcohol)

- 480ml Vodka
- 420ml Water
- 170g Sugar
- 60g Dried Plum
- 40g Acai Powder

The Process

(1) In a clean, sanitized glass jar add the vodka and plums. Seal hermetically and store in a cool, dark place for 15 days.

(2) Once the 15 days have passed, strain the liquid from the brew into a bottle and seal.

(3) Next, put a pot of water on the stove to boil. Combine the sugar and acai powder in a separate container and mix to combine. Once the water is boiling, reduce the heat to a simmer and add the acai-sugar mixture. Stir well until dissolved, then let cool.

(4) Once the acai simple syrup is cooled, add the plum vodka extract from the bottle and stir to combine.

(5) You may strain the liqueur with a fine mesh strainer or a cheese cloth to rid the mixture of any grainy residue left from the acai powder.

(6) Finally, pour the liqueur into a clean bottle and seal for 14 days.

(7) Shake well before serving. Serve cold.

41

Tropical Mix Liqueur

Ingredients
(for making 1 Liter, 18% alcohol)

- 500ml Vodka
- 460ml Water
- 4ml Organic Vanilla Extract
- 200g Sugar
- 60g Dried Cherry
- 60g Dried Strawberries
- 60g Dried Blueberries

The Process

(1) In a clean, sanitized glass jar add the vodka, cherries, strawberries, and blueberries. Seal hermetically and store in a cool, dark place for 10 days.

(2) Once the 10 days have passed, strain the liquid from the brew into a bottle and seal. Either discard the leftover berries or eat as an adult snack.

(3) Next, add the sugar and water into a pot and simmer while continuously stirring until the sugar is dissolved. Once the sugar is dissolved, add the vanilla extract. Remove from heat and allow the mixture to cool.

(4) Once the simple syrup is cooled, add the berry extract from the bottle and stir to combine.

(5) Pour the final berry mixture into a clean bottle and seal for 10 days.

(6) Shake lightly before serving. Serve cold.

Cinnamon Coconut Honey Liqueur

Ingredients
(for making 1 Liter, 19% alcohol)

- 480ml Vodka
- 400ml Water
- 130g Light Honey
- 100g Sugar
- 60g Coconut Chips
- 30g Cinnamon Sticks

The Process

(1) In a clean, sanitized glass jar add the vodka, cinnamon, and coconut chips. Seal hermetically and store in a cool, dark place for 15 days.

(2) Once the 15 days have passed, strain the liquid from the brew into a bottle and seal. Discard the leftover cinnamon sticks and coconut.

(3) Next, add the honey, sugar, and water into a pot and simmer while continuously stirring until the sugar is dissolved. Remove from heat and allow the mixture to cool.

(4) Once the simple syrup is cooled, add the cinnamon-coconut extract from the bottle and stir to combine.

(5) Pour the final mixture into a clean bottle and seal for 14 days.

(6) Shake lightly before serving. Serve cold.

Acai Plum Liqueur

Ingredients

(for making 1 Liter, 19% alcohol)

- 480ml Vodka
- 420ml Water
- 170g Sugar
- 60g Dried Plum
- 40g Acai Powder
- 40g Light Date

The Process

(1) In a clean, sanitized glass jar add the vodka, plum, and light date. Seal hermetically and store in a cool, dark place for 14 days.

(2) Once the 14 days have passed, strain the liquid from the date extract into a bottle and seal. Either discard the leftover fruit or eat as an adult snack.

(3) Next, add the sugar, acai powder, and water into a pot and simmer, continuously stirring until the acai powder and sugar have dissolved. Remove from heat and allow the mixture to cool.

(4) Once the simple syrup is cooled, add the plum extract from the bottle and stir to combine. If you notice a grainy texture from the acai powder, you can strain this off using a cheesecloth or a mesh strainer.

(5) Pour the final fruit mixture into a clean bottle and seal for 14 days.

(6) Shake before serving. Serve cold.

Nuts & Raisins Liqueur

Ingredients
(for making 1 Liter, 18.5% alcohol)

- 480ml Vodka
- 460ml Water
- 4ml Organic Vanilla Extract
- 140g Sugar
- 80g Walnuts
- 40g Cashews
- 40g Dark Raisins
- 25g Brazil Nuts

The Process

(1) In a clean, sanitized glass jar add the vodka, raisins, and nuts. Seal hermetically and store in a cool, dark place for 14 days.

(2) Once the 14 days have passed, strain the liquid from the brew into a bottle and seal. Discard the leftover raisins and nuts.

(3) Next, add the sugar and water into a pot and simmer while continuously stirring until the sugar is dissolved. Once the sugar is dissolved, stir in the vanilla extract. Remove from heat and let cool.

(4) Once the simple syrup is cooled, add the raisin-nut extract from the bottle and stir to combine.

(5) Pour the final mixture into a clean bottle and seal for 14 days.

(6) Shake lightly before serving. Serve cold.

Raspberry Cherry Liqueur

Ingredients
(for making 1 Liter, 20% alcohol)

- 520ml Vodka
- 400ml Water
- 130g Sugar
- 120g Dried Cherry
- 80g Dried Raspberries
- 40g Black Raisins

The Process

(1) In a clean, sanitized glass jar add the vodka, cherries, raspberries, and black raisins. Seal hermetically and store in a cool, dark place for 10 days.

(2) Once the 10 days have passed, strain the liquid from the brew into a bottle and seal. Feel free to eat the leftover fruit as an adult snack.

(3) Next, add the sugar and water into a pot and simmer while continuously stirring until the sugar is dissolved. Remove from heat and let cool.

(4) Once the simple syrup is cooled, add the fruit extract from the bottle and stir to combine.

(5) Pour the final mixture into a clean bottle and seal for 10 days.

(6) Shake before serving. Serve cold.

Nut & Cardamom Liqueur

Ingredients
(for making 1 Liter, 18.5% alcohol)

- 470ml Vodka
- 440ml Water
- 4ml Organic Vanilla Extract
- 160g Sugar
- 60g Pecan Nuts
- 60g Walnuts
- 40g Brazil Nuts
- 2g Ground Cardamom Powder

The Process

(1) In a clean, sanitized glass jar add the vodka, nuts, and cardamom. Seal hermetically and store in a cool, dark place for 20 days.

(2) Once the 20 days have passed, strain the liquid using a cheesecloth, pour the nut extract into a bottle and seal. Discard the leftover nuts and cardamom powder.

(3) Next, add the sugar and water into a pot and simmer while continuously stirring until the sugar is dissolved. Once the sugar is dissolved, add the vanilla extract. Remove from heat and let cool.

(4) Once the simple syrup is cooled, add the nut extract from the bottle and stir to combine.

(5) Pour the final mixture into a clean bottle and seal for 14 days.

(6) Shake before serving. Serve cold.

Passion Fruit Pineapple Liqueur

Ingredients
(for making 1 Liter, 20% alcohol)

- 500ml Vodka
- 100ml Water
- 300ml Passion Fruit Juice
- 160g Sugar
- 100g Dried Pineapple
- 40g Light Raisins

The Process

(1) In a clean, sanitized glass jar add the vodka, pineapple, and raisins. Seal hermetically and store in a cool, dark place for 10 days.

(2) Once the 10 days have passed, strain the liquid from the brew into a bottle and seal. Feel free to eat the leftover fruit as an adult snack.

(3) Next, add the sugar and water into a pot and simmer while continuously stirring until the sugar is dissolved. Once the sugar is dissolved, add the passion fruit juice. Remove from heat and let cool.

(4) Once the simple syrup is cooled, add the pineapple extract from the bottle and stir to combine.

(5) Pour the final mixture into a clean bottle and seal for 10 days.

(6) Shake before serving. Serve cold.

Mango Passion Fruit Liqueur

Ingredients
(for making 1 Liter, 18% alcohol)

• 500ml Vodka
• 400ml Passion Fruit Juice
• 100ml Water
• 150g Sugar
• 100g Dried Mango

The Process

(1) In a clean, sanitized glass jar add the mango and vodka. Seal hermetically and store in a cool, dark place for 10 days.

(2) Once the 10 days have passed, strain the liquid from mango extract into a bottle and seal. Feel free to eat the leftover fruit as an adult snack.

(3) Next, add the passion fruit juice, sugar, and water into a pot and simmer while continuously stirring until the sugar is dissolved. Remove from heat and let cool.

(4) Once the simple syrup is cooled, add the mango extract from the bottle and stir to combine.

(5) Pour the final mixture into a clean bottle and seal for 7 days.

(6) Shake lightly before serving. Serve cold.

Blueberry Mint Liqueur

Ingredients
(for making 1 Liter, 18% alcohol)

- 460ml Vodka
- 470ml Water
- 2ml Organic Vanilla Extract
- 200g Blueberries
- 120g Sugar
- 40g Mint Leaves

The Process

(1) In a clean, sanitized glass jar add the mint, blueberries, and vodka. Seal hermetically and store in a cool, dark place for 10 days.

(2) Once the 10 days have passed, strain the liquid from blueberry extract into a bottle and seal. Feel free to eat the leftover fruit as an adult snack.

(3) Next, add the sugar and water into a pot and simmer while continuously stirring until the sugar is dissolved. Once the sugar is dissolved, add the vanilla extract. Remove from heat and let cool.

(4) Once the simple syrup is cooled, add the blueberry extract from the bottle and stir to combine.

(5) Pour the final mixture into a clean bottle and seal for 14 days.

(6) Shake lightly before serving. Serve cold.

Star Anise Coconut Liqueur

Ingredients

(for making 1 Liter, 19% alcohol)

- 500ml Vodka
- 400ml Water
- 2ml Organic Vanilla Extract
- 160g Sugar
- 120g Coconut Chips
- 60g Star Anise

The Process

(1) In a clean, sanitized glass jar add the coconut chips, star anise, and vodka. Seal hermetically and store in a cool, dark place for 15 days.

(2) Once the 15 days have passed, strain the liquid from the brew into a bottle and seal. Discard any leftover coconut and anise.

(3) Next, add the sugar and water into a pot and simmer while continuously stirring until the sugar is dissolved. Once the sugar is dissolved, add the vanilla extract. Remove from heat and allow the mixture to cool.

(4) Once the simple syrup is cooled, add the coconut-anise extract from the bottle and stir to combine.

(5) Pour the final mixture into a clean bottle and seal for 14 days.

(6) Shake lightly before serving. Serve cold.

Grapefruit Pineapple Liqueur

Ingredients
(for making 1 Liter, 18% alcohol)

- 490ml Vodka
- 420ml Water
- 170g Sugar
- 200g Grapefruit Slices
- 120g Dried Pineapple
- 60g Cranberries

The Process

(1) In a clean, sanitized glass jar add the grapefruit, pineapple, cranberries, and vodka. Seal hermetically and store in a cool, dark place for 10 days.

(2) Once the 10 days have passed, strain the liquid into a bottle and seal. Feel free to eat any remaining fruit as an adult snack.

(3) Next, add the sugar and water into a pot and simmer while continuously stirring until the sugar is dissolved. Remove from heat and allow the mixture to cool.

(4) Once the simple syrup is cooled, add the grapefruit-pineapple extract from the bottle and stir to combine.

(5) Pour the final mixture into a clean bottle and seal for 10 days.

(6) Shake lightly before serving. Serve cold.

Honey & Lemon Liqueur

Ingredients
(for making 1 Liter, 19% alcohol)

- 500ml Vodka
- 350ml Water
- 200g Honey
- 90g Sugar
- 40g Fresh Lemon Peels

The Process

(1) In a clean, sanitized glass jar add the lemon peels and vodka. Seal hermetically and store in a cool, dark place for 15 days.

(2) Once the 15 days have passed, strain the liquid from the brew into a bottle and seal. Discard any leftover peels.

(3) Next, add the sugar, honey, and water into a pot and simmer while continuously stirring until the sugar is dissolved. Remove from heat and allow the mixture to cool.

(4) Once the honey syrup is cooled, add the lemon extract from the bottle and stir to combine.

(5) Pour the final mixture into a clean bottle and seal for 14 days.

(6) Shake lightly before serving. Serve cold.

Cherry Cinnamon Liqueur

Ingredients
(for making 1 Liter, 20% alcohol)

- 500ml Vodka
- 600ml Water
- 4ml Organic Vanilla Extract
- 200g Sugar
- 160g Dried Cherry
- 50g Cinnamon Sticks

The Process

(1) In a clean, sanitized glass jar add the dried cherries, cinnamon sticks, and vodka. Seal hermetically and store in a cool, dark place for 15 days.

(2) Once the 15 days have passed, strain the liquid from the brew into a bottle and seal. Discard the cinnamon sticks but feel free to eat the cherries.

(3) Next, add the sugar and water into a pot and simmer while continuously stirring until the sugar is dissolved. Once the sugar is dissolved, add the vanilla extract. Remove from heat and let cool.

(4) Once the simple syrup is cooled, add the cherry-cinnamon extract from the bottle and stir to combine.

(5) Pour the final mixture into a clean bottle and seal for 14 days.

(6) Shake lightly before serving. Serve cold.

Perfumed Honey Liqueur

Ingredients
(for making 1 Liter, 18% alcohol)

- 460ml Vodka
- 340ml Water
- 200g Light Honey
- 4g Rosemary Leaves
- 4g Broken Cardamom
- 2g Lemon Verbena Leaves

The Process

(1) In a metal pot, add the water, rosemary, cardamom, and lemon verbena and boil for 2 minutes. Strain the leaves.

(2) Next, add the honey to the pot and stir until it is evenly incorporated with the herbal water (do not boil).

(3) Once the simple syrup is cooled, add the vodka and stir to combine.

(4) Pour the final mixture into a clean bottle and seal for 14 days.

(5) Shake lightly before serving. Serve cold.

Banana Melon Liqueur

Ingredients

(for making 1 Liter, 18% alcohol)

- 460ml Vodka
- 440ml Water
- 4ml Organic Vanilla Extract
- 160g Sugar
- 120g Dried Melon
- 120g Dried Banana

The Process

(1) In a clean, sanitized glass jar add the melon, banana, and vodka. Seal hermetically and store in a cool, dark place for 10 days.

(2) Once the 10 days have passed, strain the liquid from the brew into a bottle and seal. Feel free to eat the leftover fruit as an adult snack.

(3) Next, add the sugar and water into a pot and simmer while continuously stirring until the sugar is dissolved. Once the sugar is dissolved, add the vanilla extract. Remove from heat and allow the mixture to cool.

(4) Once the simple syrup is cooled, add the banana-melon extract from the bottle and stir to combine.

(5) Pour the final mixture into a clean bottle and seal for 10 days.

(6) Shake lightly before serving. Serve cold.

Mango Banana Liqueur

Ingredients

(for making 1 Liter, 18% alcohol)

• 490ml Vodka
• 490ml Water
• 2ml Organic Vanilla Extract
• 160g Sugar
• 100g Dried Mango
• 100g Fresh Banana (peeled)

The Process

(1) In a clean, sanitized glass jar add the dried mango, fresh banana slices, and vodka. Seal hermetically and store in a cool, dark place for 10 days.

(2) Once the 10 days have passed, strain the liquid from the brew into a bottle and seal. Discard any leftover banana but feel free to eat the mango as it has now absorbed some of the vodka.

(3) Next, add the sugar and water into a pot and simmer while continuously stirring until the sugar is dissolved. Once the sugar is dissolved, add the vanilla extract. Remove from heat and allow the mixture to cool.

(4) Once the simple syrup is cooled, add the mango-banana extract from the bottle and stir to combine.

(5) Pour the final mixture into a clean bottle and seal for 10 days.

(6) Shake lightly before serving. Serve cold.

Mango Blueberry Liqueur

Ingredients
(for making 1 Liter, 19% alcohol)

- 500ml Vodka
- 420ml Water
- 4ml Organic Vanilla Extract
- 180g Sugar
- 100g Dried Mango
- 60g Blueberries

The Process

(1) In a clean, sanitized glass jar add the mango, blueberries, and vodka. Seal hermetically and store in a cool, dark place for 10 days.

(2) Once the 10 days have passed, strain the liquid from the mango-blueberry extract into a bottle and seal. Discard any leftover blueberries but feel free to eat the mango as it has now absorbed the vodka.

(3) Next, add the sugar and water into a pot and simmer while continuously stirring until the sugar is dissolved. Once the sugar is dissolved, add the vanilla extract. Remove from heat and allow the mixture to cool.

(4) Once the simple syrup is cooled, add the mango-blueberry extract from the bottle and stir to combine.

(5) Pour the final mixture into a clean bottle and seal for 10 days.

(6) Shake lightly before serving. Serve cold.

Blackberry Blueberry Liqueur

Ingredients
(for making 1 Liter, 19% alcohol)

- 490ml Vodka
- 420ml Water
- 6ml Organic Vanilla Extract
- 160g Sugar
- 120g Blackberry
- 100g Blueberry
- 60g Dark Raisin

The Process

(1) In a clean, sanitized glass jar add the blackberries, blueberries, dark raisins, and vodka. Seal hermetically and store in a cool, dark place for 10 days.

(2) Once the 10 days have passed, strain the liquid into a bottle and seal. Either discard any leftover fruit or blend it up into an adult smoothie.

(3) Next, add the sugar and water into a pot and simmer while continuously stirring until the sugar is dissolved. Once the sugar is dissolved, add the vanilla extract. Remove from heat and allow the mixture to cool.

(4) Once the simple syrup is cooled, add the berry extract from the bottle and stir to combine.

(5) Pour the final mixture into a clean bottle and seal for 10 days.

(6) Shake lightly before serving. Serve cold.

Coconut Pineapple Ginger Liqueur

Ingredients

(for making 1 Liter, 20% alcohol)

- 500ml Vodka
- 400ml Water
- 160g Sugar
- 100g Dried Ginger
- 60g Coconut Chips
- 40g Dried Pineapple

The Process

(1) In a clean, sanitized glass jar add the coconut chips, ginger, pineapple, and vodka. Seal hermetically and store in a cool, dark place for 10 days.

(2) Once the 10 days have passed, strain the liquid from the brew into a bottle and seal. Discard any leftover coconut, but feel free to eat or blend up the leftover ginger and pineapple as a smoothie.

(3) Next, add the sugar and water into a pot and simmer while continuously stirring until the sugar is dissolved. Remove from heat and allow the mixture to cool.

(4) Once the simple syrup is cooled, add the coconut-pineapple extract from the bottle and stir to combine.

(5) Pour the final mixture into a clean bottle and seal for 10 days.

(6) Shake lightly before serving. Serve cold.

Cinnamon & Clove Liqueur

Ingredients
(for making 1 Liter, 19% alcohol)

- 500ml Vodka
- 440ml Water
- 4ml Organic Vanilla Extract
- 160g Sugar
- 40g Cinnamon Sticks
- 40g Coconut Chips
- 1g Whole Cloves

The Process

(1) In a clean, sanitized glass jar add the coconut chips, cinnamon sticks, cloves, and vodka. Seal hermetically and store in a cool, dark place for 14 days.

(2) Once the 14 days have passed, strain the liquid from the brew into a bottle and seal. Discard any leftover spices.

(3) Next, add the sugar and water into a pot and simmer while continuously stirring until the sugar is dissolved. Once the sugar is dissolved, add the vanilla extract. Remove from heat and allow the mixture to cool.

(4) Once the simple syrup is cooled, add the cinnamon-clove extract from the bottle and stir to combine.

(5) Pour the final mixture into a clean bottle and seal for 14 days.

(6) Shake lightly before serving. Serve cold.

Coconut Honey Liqueur

Ingredients

(for making 1 Liter, 19% alcohol)

- 490ml Vodka
- 380ml Water
- 100g Sugar
- 120g Coconut Chips
- 80g Cranberries
- 80g Honey

The Process

(1) In a clean, sanitized glass jar add the coconut chips, cranberries, and vodka. Seal hermetically and store in a cool, dark place for 15 days.

(2) Once the 15 days have passed, strain the liquid from the brew into a bottle and seal. Discard any leftover coconut and cranberry.

(3) Next, add the honey, sugar and water into a pot and simmer while continuously stirring until the sugar is dissolved. Do not boil this mixture, as it will affect the honey. Remove from heat and let cool.

(4) Once the simple syrup is cooled, add the coconut-cranberry extract from the bottle and stir to combine.

(5) Pour the final mixture into a clean bottle and seal for 14 days.

(6) Shake lightly before serving. Serve cold.

Coconut Pineapple Liqueur

Ingredients

(for making 1 Liter, 19% alcohol)

- 480ml Vodka
- 400ml Water
- 4ml Organic Vanilla Extract
- 180g Sugar
- 160g Dried Pineapple
- 120g Coconut chips
- 40g Light Raisins

The Process

(1) In a clean, sanitized glass jar add the coconut chips, pineapple, raisins, and vodka. Seal hermetically and store in a cool, dark place for 14 days.

(2) Once the 14 days have passed, strain the liquid from the brew into a bottle and seal. Discard any leftover coconut, but feel free to eat the pineapple and raisins.

(3) Next, add the sugar and water into a pot and simmer while continuously stirring until the sugar is dissolved. Once the sugar is dissolved, add the vanilla extract. Remove from heat and allow the mixture to cool.

(4) Once the simple syrup is cooled, add the coconut-pineapple extract from the bottle and stir to combine.

(5) Pour the final mixture into a clean bottle and seal for 14 days.

(6) Shake lightly before serving. Serve cold.

Coconut Peach Liqueur

Ingredients
(for making 1 Liter, 19% alcohol)

- 500ml Vodka
- 420ml Water
- 4ml Organic Vanilla Extract
- 160g Sugar
- 160g Coconut Chips
- 120g Dried Peach

The Process

(1) In a clean, sanitized glass jar add the coconut chips, peach, and vodka. Seal hermetically and store in a cool, dark place for 14 days.

(2) Once the 14 days have passed, strain the liquid from the brew into a bottle and seal. Discard any leftover coconut, but feel free to eat the peach.

(3) Next, add the sugar and water into a pot and simmer while continuously stirring until the sugar is dissolved. Once the sugar is dissolved, add the vanilla extract. Remove from heat and allow the mixture to cool.

(4) Once the simple syrup is cooled, add the coconut-peach extract from the bottle and stir to combine.

(5) Pour the final mixture into a clean bottle and seal for 14 days.

(6) Shake lightly before serving. Serve cold.

Pineapple Kiwi Liqueur

Ingredients
(for making 1 Liter, 18% alcohol)

- 480ml Vodka
- 460ml Water
- 120g Sugar
- 160g Dried Kiwi
- 80g Dried Pineapple
- 40g Light Raisins

The Process

(1) In a clean, sanitized glass jar add the kiwi, pineapple, raisins, and vodka. Seal hermetically and store in a cool, dark place for 10 days.

(2) Once the 10 days have passed, strain the liquid from the brew into a bottle and seal. Feel free to eat any leftover fruit.

(3) Next, add the sugar and water into a pot and simmer while continuously stirring until the sugar is dissolved. Remove from heat and allow the mixture to cool.

(4) Once the simple syrup is cooled, add the pineapple-kiwi extract from the bottle and stir to combine.

(5) Pour the final mixture into a clean bottle and seal for 10 days.

(6) Shake lightly before serving. Serve cold.

Cinnamon & Ginger Liqueur

Ingredients
(for making 1 Liter, 19% alcohol)

- 480ml Vodka
- 440ml Water
- 4ml Organic Vanilla Extract
- 160g Sugar
- 60g Fresh Ground Ginger
- 20g Broken Cinnamon Sticks

The Process

(1) In a clean, sanitized glass jar add the cinnamon sticks, ginger, and vodka. Seal hermetically and store in a cool, dark place for 15 days.

(2) Once the 15 days have passed, strain the liquid from the brew into a bottle and seal. Discard any leftover ginger and cinnamon.

(3) Next, add the sugar and water into a pot and simmer while continuously stirring until the sugar is dissolved. Once the sugar is dissolved, add the vanilla extract. Remove from heat and allow the mixture to cool.

(4) Once the simple syrup is cooled, add the cinnamon-ginger extract from the bottle and stir to combine.

(5) Pour the final mixture into a clean bottle and seal for 14 days.

(7) Shake lightly before serving. Serve cold.

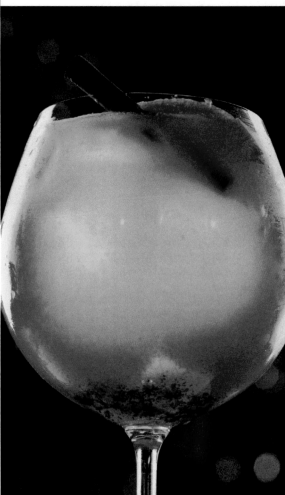

Coconut Chocolate Liqueur

Ingredients

(for making 1 Liter, 17.5% alcohol)

- 480ml Vodka
- 200ml Water
- 280ml Coconut Cream
- 8ml Organic Vanilla Extract
- 180g Sugar
- 60g Powdered Milk
- 8g Dark Cocoa Powder

The Process

(1) In a clean bowl add the cocoa powder, powdered milk, and sugar. Stir until evenly incorporated.

(2) Next, add the water to a metal pot and bring to a boil. Pour the boiling water over the powdered mixture and mix until the sugar is dissolved.

(3) Once the sugar is dissolved, add the vanilla extract and coconut cream. Remove from heat and allow the mixture to cool.

(4) Once the cocoa mixture has cooled, strain through a mesh strainer or cheesecloth to ensure it is as smooth as possible. Once you have strained the mixture, add the vodka and mix to combine.

(5) Pour the cocoa mixture into bottles and seal hermetically for 14 days.

(6) Shake lightly before serving. Serve cold.

Plum & Raisin Liqueur

Ingredients
(for making 1 Liter, 19% alcohol)

- 500ml Vodka
- 420ml Water
- 4ml Organic Vanilla Extract
- 180g Sugar
- 140g Dried Plums
- 80g Dark Raisins

The Process

(1) In a clean, sanitized glass jar add the plums, raisins, and vodka. Seal hermetically and store in a cool, dark place for 10 days.

(2) Once the 10 days have passed, strain the liquid from plum extract into a bottle and seal. Feel free to eat any of the plums and raisins.

(3) Next, add the sugar and water into a pot and simmer while continuously stirring until the sugar is dissolved. Once the sugar is dissolved, add the vanilla extract. Remove from heat and allow the mixture to cool.

(4) Once the simple syrup is cooled, add the plum extract from the bottle and stir to combine.

(5) Pour the final mixture into a clean bottle and seal for 10 days.

(6) Shake lightly before serving. Serve cold.

Acai &
Carob Liqueur

Ingredients
(for making 1 Liter, 19% alcohol)

• 480ml Vodka
• 420ml Water
• 170g Sugar
• 40g Acai Powder
• 40g Carob Powder

The Process

(1) Fill a metal pot with water and bring to a boil. In a separate bowl combine your acai powder, carob powder, and sugar.

(2) Add in your boiling water and stir until the sugar is dissolved. Cover and allow the mixture to cool and the flavors to meld together.

(3) Once the mixture has cooled, stir in the vodka and pour into a clean bottle. Seal for 10 days.

(4) Once the 10 days have passed, add the plum extract from the bottle and stir to combine.

(5) Shake before serving. Serve cold.

Coconut Cherry Liqueur

Ingredients
(for making 1 Liter, 20% alcohol)

- 520ml Vodka
- 420ml Water
- 140g Sugar
- 100g Coconut Chips
- 80g Dried Cherry

The Process

(1) In a clean, sanitized glass jar add the coconut chips, cherry, and vodka. Seal hermetically and store in a cool, dark place for 15 days.

(2) Once the 15 days have passed, strain the liquid from the brew into a bottle and seal. Discard any leftover coconut, but feel free to eat the cherries.

(3) Next, add the sugar and water into a pot and simmer while continuously stirring until the sugar is dissolved. Remove from heat and allow the mixture to cool.

(4) Once the simple syrup is cooled, add the coconut-cherry extract from the bottle and stir to combine.

(5) Pour the final mixture into a clean bottle and seal for 14 days.

(6) Shake before serving. Serve cold.

Strawberry Banana Liqueur

Ingredients
(for making 1 Liter, 18% alcohol)

- 480ml Vodka
- 410ml Water
- 4ml Organic Vanilla Extract
- 180g Sugar
- 100g Fresh Strawberries
- 80g Fresh Banana (peeled)

The Process

(1) In a clean, sanitized glass jar add the strawberries, sliced banana, and vodka. Seal hermetically and store in a cool, dark place for 10 days.

(2) Once the 10 days have passed, strain the liquid from the brew into a bottle and seal. Feel free to blend up the leftover fruit into an adult smoothie, but after you remove the banana skin.

(3) Next, add the sugar and water into a pot and simmer while continuously stirring until the sugar is dissolved. Once the sugar is dissolved, add the vanilla extract. Remove from heat and let cool.

(4) Once the simple syrup is cooled, add the strawberry-banana extract from the bottle and stir to combine.

(5) Pour the final mixture into a clean bottle and seal for 10 days.

(6) Shake before serving. Serve cold.

Date, Apple & Cinnamon Liqueur

Ingredients
(for making 1 Liter, 18% alcohol)

- 480ml Vodka
- 450ml Water
- 180g Sugar
- 200g Dried Apple
- 150g Fresh Dates
- 6g Cinnamon Sticks

The Process

(1) In a clean, sanitized glass jar add the apple, dates, cinnamon sticks, and vodka. Seal hermetically and store in a cool, dark place for 15 days.

(2) Once the 15 days have passed, strain the liquid from the brew into a bottle and seal. Discard any leftover cinnamon sticks, but feel free to eat the apples and dates.

(3) Next, add the sugar and water into a pot and simmer while continuously stirring until the sugar is dissolved. Remove from heat and allow the mixture to cool.

(4) Once the simple syrup is cooled, add the apple-cinnamon extract from the bottle and stir to combine.

(5) Pour the final mixture into a clean bottle and seal for 7 days.

(6) Shake before serving. Serve cold.

Strawberry Raisin Liqueur

Ingredients

(for making 1 Liter, 19% alcohol)

- 480ml Vodka
- 410ml Water
- 4ml Organic Vanilla Extract
- 180g Sugar
- 200g Fresh Strawberries
- 40g Black Raisins

The Process

(1) In a clean, sanitized glass jar add the strawberries, raisins, and vodka. Seal hermetically and store in a cool, dark place for 10 days.

(2) Once the 10 days have passed, strain the liquid from the brew into a bottle and seal. Feel free to eat the raisins or blend the fruit to make an adult strawberry smoothie.

(3) Next, add the sugar and water into a pot and simmer while continuously stirring until the sugar is dissolved. Once the sugar is dissolved, add the vanilla extract. Remove from heat and allow the mixture to cool.

(4) Once the simple syrup is cooled, add the strawberry-raisin extract from the bottle and stir to combine.

(5) Pour the final mixture into a clean bottle and seal for 10 days.

(6) Shake before serving. Serve cold.

Pineapple Orange Liqueur

Ingredients
(for making 1 Liter, 18% alcohol)

- 580ml Vodka
- 360ml Water
- 160g Sugar
- 160g Orange Slices
- 120g Dried Pineapple

The Process

(1) In a clean, sanitized glass jar add the pineapple, orange slices, and vodka. Seal hermetically and store in a cool, dark place for 10 days.

(2) Once the 10 days have passed, strain the liquid from the brew into a bottle and seal. Do not squeeze the fruit pulp, as it will make the drink bitter. Feel free to eat the leftover pineapple and orange.

(3) Next, add the sugar and water into a pot and simmer while continuously stirring until the sugar is dissolved. Remove from heat and allow the mixture to cool.

(4) Once the simple syrup is cooled, add the pineapple-orange extract from the bottle and stir to combine.

(5) Pour the final mixture into a clean bottle and seal for 10 days.

(6) Shake before serving. Serve cold.

Coconut & Goji Liqueur

Ingredients
(for making 1 Liter, 20% alcohol)

• 550ml Vodka
• 400ml Water
• 200g Sugar
• 300g Dried Goji Berry
• 100g Coconut Chips

The Process

(1) In a clean, sanitized glass jar add the goji berry, coconut chips, and vodka. Seal hermetically and store in a cool, dark place for 10 days.

(2) Once the 10 days have passed, strain the liquid from the brew into a bottle and seal. Discard any leftover coconut, but feel free to eat the goji berries.

(3) Next, add the sugar and water into a pot and simmer while continuously stirring until the sugar is dissolved. Remove from heat and allow the mixture to cool.

(4) Once the simple syrup is cooled, add the coconut-goji extract from the bottle and stir to combine.

(5) Pour the final mixture into a clean bottle and seal for 10 days.

(6) Shake before serving. Serve cold.

Strawberry Kiwi Liqueur

Ingredients

(for making 1 Liter, 19% alcohol)

- 500ml Vodka
- 420ml Water
- 4ml Organic Vanilla Extract
- 160g Sugar
- 160g Dried Kiwi
- 180g Strawberries
- 40g Light Raisin

The Process

(1) In a clean, sanitized glass jar add the kiwi, strawberries, raisin, and vodka. Seal hermetically and store in a cool, dark place for 10 days.

(2) Once the 10 days have passed, Strain the liquid from the brew into a bottle and seal. Feel free to blend up the fruit into an adult smoothie.

(3) Next, add the sugar and water into a pot and simmer while continuously stirring until the sugar is dissolved. Once the sugar is dissolved, add the vanilla extract. Remove from heat and allow the mixture to cool.

(4) Once the simple syrup is cooled, add the strawberry-kiwi extract from the bottle and stir to combine.

(5) Pour the final mixture into a clean bottle and seal for 10 days.

(6) Shake before serving. Serve cold.

Pineapple Apple Liqueur

Ingredients

(for making 1 Liter, 19% alcohol)

- 500ml Vodka
- 420ml Water
- 4ml Organic Vanilla Extract
- 160g Sugar
- 120g Dried Apple
- 120g Dried Pineapple
- 40g Light Raisins

The Process

(1) In a clean, sanitized glass jar add the apple, pineapple, raisins, and vodka. Seal hermetically and store in a cool, dark place for 10 days.

(2) Once the 10 days have passed, strain the liquid from the brew into a bottle and seal. Feel free to eat the leftover fruit as an adult snack.

(3) Next, add the sugar and water into a pot and simmer while continuously stirring until the sugar is dissolved. Once the sugar is dissolved, add the vanilla extract. Remove from heat and allow the mixture to cool.

(4) Once the simple syrup is cooled, add the pineapple-apple extract from the bottle and stir to combine.

(5) Pour the final mixture into a clean bottle and seal for 10 days.

(6) Shake before serving. Serve cold.

Apple Cardamom Liqueur

Ingredients
(for making 1 Liter, 18% alcohol)

- 520ml Vodka
- 380ml Water
- 8ml Organic Vanilla Extract
- 160g Sugar
- 140g Dried Apple Slices
- 2g Ground Cardamom

The Process

(1) In a clean, sanitized glass jar add the apple, cardamom, and vodka. Seal hermetically and store in a cool, dark place for 14 days.

(2) Once the 14 days have passed, strain the liquid from the brew into a bottle and seal. Discard any leftover cardamom, but feel free to eat the apple slices.

(3) Next, add the sugar and water into a pot and simmer while continuously stirring until the sugar is dissolved. Once the sugar is dissolved, add the vanilla extract. Remove from heat and allow the mixture to cool.

(4) Once the simple syrup is cooled, add the apple-cardamom extract from the bottle and stir to combine.

(5) Pour the final mixture into a clean bottle and seal for 10 days.

(6) Shake before serving. Serve cold.

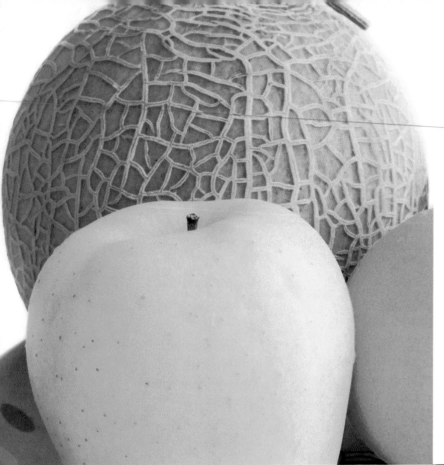

Apple Melon Liqueur

Ingredients
(for making 1 Liter, 19% alcohol)

- 460ml Vodka
- 440ml Water
- 4ml Organic Vanilla Extract
- 180g Sugar
- 120g Dried Melon
- 100g Dried Apple

The Process

(1) In a clean, sanitized glass jar add the apple, melon, and vodka. Seal hermetically and store in a cool, dark place for 10 days.

(2) Once the 10 days have passed, strain the liquid from the brew into a bottle and seal.

(3) Next, add the sugar and water into a pot and simmer while continuously stirring until the sugar is dissolved. Once the sugar is dissolved, add the vanilla extract. Remove from heat and allow the mixture to cool.

(4) Once the simple syrup is cooled, add the apple-melon extract from the bottle and stir to combine.

(5) Pour the final mixture into a clean bottle and seal for 10 days.

(6) Shake lightly before serving. Serve cold.

Apple Ginger Liqueur

Ingredients

(for making 1 Liter, 19% alcohol)

• 520ml Vodka
• 240ml Water
• 200g Sugar
• 140g Dried Apples
• 40g Fresh Ginger

The Process

(1) In a clean, sanitized glass jar add the apple, ginger, and vodka. Seal hermetically and store in a cool, dark place for 14 days.

(2) Once the 14 days have passed, strain the liquid from the brew into a bottle and seal. Discard any leftover ginger, but feel free to eat the apples.

(3) Next, add the sugar and water into a pot and simmer while continuously stirring until the sugar is dissolved. Remove from heat and allow the mixture to cool.

(4) Once the simple syrup is cooled, add the apple-ginger extract from the bottle and stir to combine.

(5) Pour the final mixture into a clean bottle and seal for 14 days.

(6) Shake before serving. Serve cold.

Apple Date Liqueur

Ingredients

(for making 1 Liter, 19% alcohol)

- 480ml Vodka
- 420ml Water
- 4ml Organic Vanilla Extract
- 160g Sugar
- 160g Dried Apple
- 100g Dates

The Process

(1) In a clean, sanitized glass jar add the apple, dates, and vodka. Seal hermetically and store in a cool, dark place for 10 days.

(2) Once the 10 days have passed, strain the liquid from the brew into a bottle and seal. Feel free to eat the apples and dates as an adult snack.

(3) Next, add the sugar and water into a pot and simmer while continuously stirring until the sugar is dissolved. Once the sugar is dissolved, add the vanilla extract. Remove from heat and allow the mixture to cool.

(4) Once the simple syrup is cooled, add the apple-date extract from the bottle and stir to combine.

(5) Pour the final mixture into a clean bottle and seal for 10 days.

(6) Shake before serving. Serve cold.

Mango Pineapple Liqueur

Ingredients
(for making 1 Liter, 18% alcohol)

- 460ml Vodka
- 430ml Water
- 170g Sugar
- 100g Dried Mango
- 80g Dried Pineapple
- 40g Light Raisins

The Process

(1) In a clean, sanitized glass jar add the mango, pineapple, raisins, and vodka. Seal hermetically and store in a cool, dark place for 10 days.

(2) Once the 10 days have passed, strain the liquid from the brew into a bottle and seal. Feel free to eat the leftover fruit as an adult snack.

(3) Next, add the sugar and water into a pot and simmer while continuously stirring until the sugar is dissolved. Remove from heat and allow the mixture to cool.

(4) Once the simple syrup is cooled, add the mango-pineapple extract from the bottle and stir to combine.

(5) Pour the final mixture into a clean bottle and seal for 10 days.

(6) Shake before serving. Serve cold.

Nuts & Sesame Liqueur

Ingredients
(for making 1 Liter, 18% alcohol)

- 460ml Vodka
- 440ml Water
- 4ml Organic Vanilla Extract
- 40g Pecans
- 160g Sugar
- 40g Almonds
- 60g Walnuts
- 60g Cashews
- 20g Sesame Seeds
- 40g Dark Raisins

The Process

(1) In a clean, sanitized glass jar add the nuts, raisins, sesame seeds, and vodka. Seal hermetically and store in a cool, dark place for 15 days.

(2) Once the 15 days have passed, strain the liquid from the brew into a bottle and seal. Discard any leftover nuts, but feel free to eat the raisins.

(3) Next, add the sugar and water into a pot and simmer while continuously stirring until the sugar is dissolved. Once the sugar is dissolved, add the vanilla extract. Remove from heat and let cool.

(4) Once the simple syrup is cooled, add the nut extract from the bottle and stir to combine.

(5) Pour the final mixture into a clean bottle and seal for 14 days.

(6) Shake before serving. Serve cold.

Date Cardamom Liqueur

Ingredients
(for making 1 Liter, 19% alcohol)

- 500ml Vodka
- 400ml Water
- 160g Sugar
- 160g Dates
- 1g Broken Cardamom Pods

The Process

(1) In a clean, sanitized glass jar add the dates, cardamom, and vodka. Seal hermetically and store in a cool, dark place for 10 days.

(2) Once the 10 days have passed, strain the liquid from the brew into a bottle and seal. Discard any leftover cardamom pods, but feel free to eat the dates.

(3) Next, add the sugar and water into a pot and simmer while continuously stirring until the sugar is dissolved. Remove from heat and allow the mixture to cool.

(4) Once the simple syrup is cooled, add the date-cardamom extract from the bottle and stir to combine.

(5) Pour the final mixture into a clean bottle and seal for 10 days.

(6) Shake before serving. Serve cold.

Date Cocoa Liqueur

Ingredients

(for making 1 Liter, 18.5% alcohol)

- 480ml Vodka
- 440ml Water
- 4ml Organic Vanilla Extract
- 200g Dates
- 160g Sugar
- 20g Dark Raisins
- 6g Dark Cocoa Powder

The Process

(1) In a clean, sanitized glass jar add the dates, raisins, and vodka. Seal hermetically and store in a cool, dark place for 10 days.

(2) Once the 10 days have passed, strain the liquid from the brew into a bottle and seal. Feel free to eat the dates and raisins as an adult snack.

(3) Next, add the cocoa powder, sugar, and water into a pot and simmer while continuously stirring until the sugar is dissolved. Once the sugar is dissolved, add the vanilla extract. Remove from heat and allow the mixture to cool.

(4) Once the simple syrup is cooled, add the date-raisin extract from the bottle and stir to combine.

(5) Pour the final mixture into a clean bottle and seal for 10 days.

(6) Shake before serving. Serve cold.

Melon Apricot Liqueur

Ingredients
(for making 1 Liter, 19% alcohol)

- 500ml Vodka
- 40g Light Raisins
- 460ml Water
- 180g Dried Melon
- 4ml Organic Vanilla Extract
- 180g Dried Apricot
- 125g Sugar

The Process

(1) In a clean, sanitized glass jar add the apricot, melon, raisins, and vodka. Seal hermetically and store in a cool, dark place for 10 days.

(2) Once the 10 days have passed, strain the liquid from the brew into a bottle and seal. Feel free to eat the leftover fruit as an adult snack.

(3) Next, add the sugar and water into a pot and simmer while continuously stirring until the sugar is dissolved. Once the sugar is dissolved, add the vanilla extract. Remove from heat and let cool.

(4) Once the simple syrup is cooled, add the apricot-melon extract from the bottle and stir to combine.

(5) Pour the final mixture into a clean bottle and seal for 10 days.

(6) Shake before serving. Serve cold.

Coconut Cinnamon Liqueur

Ingredients

(for making 1 Liter, 18% alcohol)

- 500ml Vodka
- 400ml Water
- 160g Sugar
- 80g Dried Coconut
- 20g Cinnamon Sticks

The Process

(1) In a clean, sanitized glass jar add the coconut, cinnamon, and vodka. Seal hermetically and store in a cool, dark place for 10 days.

(2) Once the 10 days have passed, strain the liquid from the brew into a bottle and seal. Discard any leftover cinnamon and coconut.

(3) Next, add the sugar and water into a pot and simmer while continuously stirring until the sugar is dissolved. Remove from heat and allow the mixture to cool.

(4) Once the simple syrup is cooled, add the cinnamon-coconut extract from the bottle and stir to combine.

(5) Pour the final mixture into a clean bottle and seal for 14 days.

(6) Shake before serving. Serve cold.

Banana Honey Liqueur

Ingredients
(for making 1 Liter, 18% alcohol)

- 460ml Vodka
- 440ml Water
- 120g Light Honey
- 100g Sugar
- 100g Dried Banana

The Process

(1) In a clean, sanitized glass jar add the dried banana and vodka. Seal hermetically and store in a cool, dark place for 10 days.

(2) Once the 10 days have passed, strain the liquid from the brew into a bottle and seal. Discard the leftover banana or blend it into an adult banana smoothie.

(3) Next, add the honey, sugar, and water into a pot and simmer while continuously stirring until the sugar is dissolved. Do not boil this mixture, as it will affect the honey. Remove from heat and allow the mixture to cool.

(4) Once the simple syrup is cooled, add the banana extract from the bottle and stir to combine.

(5) Pour the final mixture into a clean bottle and seal for 14 days.

(6) Shake before serving. Serve cold.

Pineapple Figs Liqueur

Ingredients
(for making 1 Liter, 19% alcohol)

- 500ml Vodka
- 420ml Water
- 160g Sugar
- 160g Dried Pineapple
- 180g Dried Figs

The Process

(1) In a clean, sanitized glass jar add the pineapple, figs, and vodka. Seal hermetically and store in a cool, dark place for 10 days.

(2) Once the 10 days have passed, strain the liquid from the brew into a bottle and seal. Feel free to eat the leftover pineapple and figs as an adult snack.

(3) Next, add the sugar and water into a pot and simmer while continuously stirring until the sugar is dissolved. Remove from heat and allow the mixture to cool.

(4) Once the simple syrup is cooled, add the pineapple-fig extract from the bottle and stir to combine.

(5) Pour the final mixture into a clean bottle and seal for 10 days.

(6) Shake before serving. Serve cold.

Date & Nuts Liqueur

Ingredients
(for making 1 Liter, 19% alcohol)

• 480ml Vodka
• 400ml Water
• 4ml Organic Vanilla Extract
• 150g Sugar
• 150g Dates
• 60g Walnuts

The Process

(1) In a clean, sanitized glass jar add the dates, walnuts, and vodka. Seal hermetically and store in a cool, dark place for 15 days.

(2) Once the 15 days have passed, strain the liquid from the brew into a bottle and seal. Discard any leftover nuts, but feel free to eat the dates.

(3) Next, add the sugar and water into a pot and simmer while continuously stirring until the sugar is dissolved. Once the sugar is dissolved, add the vanilla extract. Remove from heat and allow the mixture to cool.

(4) Once the simple syrup is cooled, add the walnut-date extract from the bottle and stir to combine.

(5) Pour the final mixture into a clean bottle and seal for 14 days.

(6) Shake before serving. Serve cold.

Cinnamon Dates Liqueur

Ingredients
(for making 1 Liter, 18% alcohol)

- 460ml Vodka
- 450ml Water
- 180g Sugar
- 150g Fresh Dates
- 6g Broken Cinnamon Sticks

The Process

(1) In a clean, sanitized glass jar add the dates, cinnamon sticks, and vodka. Seal hermetically and store in a cool, dark place for 10 days.

(2) Once the 10 days have passed, strain the liquid from the brew into a bottle and seal. Discard any leftover cinnamon, but feel free to eat the dates.

(3) Next, add the sugar and water into a pot and simmer while continuously stirring until the sugar is dissolved. Remove from heat and allow the mixture to cool.

(4) Once the simple syrup is cooled, add the cinnamon-date extract from the bottle and stir to combine.

(5) Pour the final mixture into a clean bottle and seal for 14 days.

(6) Shake before serving. Serve cold.

Goji Berry Plum Liqueur

Ingredients

(for making 1 Liter, 19% alcohol)

- 500ml Vodka
- 420ml Water
- 180g Sugar
- 100g Goji Berry
- 80g Plums

The Process

(1) In a clean, sanitized glass jar add the goji berries, plums, and vodka. Seal hermetically and store in a cool, dark place for 10 days.

(2) Once the 10 days have passed, strain the liquid from goji-plum extract into a bottle and seal. Feel free to eat the goji berries and plums.

(3) Next, add the sugar and water into a pot and simmer while continuously stirring until the sugar is dissolved. Remove from heat and allow the mixture to cool.

(4) Once the simple syrup is cooled, add the goji-plum extract from the bottle and stir to combine.

(5) Pour the final mixture into a clean bottle and seal for seven days.

(6) Shake before serving. Serve cold.

Apricot Banana Liqueur

Ingredients
(for making 1 Liter, 19% alcohol)

- 500ml Vodka
- 400ml Water
- 200g Sugar
- 100g Dried Apricot
- 150g Dried Banana
- 60g Light Raisins

The Process

(1) In a clean, sanitized glass jar add the apricot, banana, raisins, and vodka. Seal hermetically and store in a cool, dark place for 10 days.

(2) Once the 10 days have passed, strain the liquid from the brew into a bottle and seal. Discard any leftover bananas, but feel free to eat the apricot and raisins.

(3) Next, add the sugar and water into a pot and simmer while continuously stirring until the sugar is dissolved. Remove from heat and allow the mixture to cool.

(4) Once the simple syrup is cooled, add the apricot-banana extract from the bottle and stir to combine.

(5) Pour the final mixture into a clean bottle and seal for 10 days.

(6) Shake before serving. Serve cold.

Marula Apricot Liqueur

Ingredients

(for making 1 Liter, 20% alcohol)

- 520ml Vodka
- 400ml Water
- 180g Sugar
- 200g Marula
- 120g Dried Apricot
- 40g Light Raisins

The Process

(1) In a clean, sanitized glass jar add the marula, apricot, raisins, and vodka. Seal hermetically and store in a cool, dark place for 10 days.

(2) Once the 10 days have passed, strain the liquid from the brew into a bottle and seal. Feel free to eat the leftover fruit.

(3) Next, add the sugar and water into a pot and simmer while continuously stirring until the sugar is dissolved. Remove from heat and allow the mixture to cool.

(4) Once the simple syrup is cooled, add the marula-apricot extract from the bottle and stir to combine.

(5) Pour the final mixture into a clean bottle and seal for 14 days.

(6) Shake before serving. Serve cold.

Fig & Kiwi Liqueur

Ingredients
(for making 1 Liter, 19% alcohol)

- 500ml Vodka
- 420ml Water
- 160g Sugar
- 160g Dried Figs
- 140g Dried Kiwi

The Process

(1) In a clean, sanitized glass jar add the kiwi, figs, and vodka. Seal hermetically and store in a cool, dark place for 10 days.

(2) Once the 10 days have passed, strain the liquid from the brew into a bottle and seal. Feel free to eat the leftover fruit as an adult snack.

(3) Next, add the sugar and water into a pot and simmer while continuously stirring until the sugar is dissolved. Remove from heat and allow the mixture to cool.

(4) Once the simple syrup is cooled, add the kiwi-fig extract from the bottle and stir to combine.

(5) Pour the final mixture into a clean bottle and seal for 10 days.

(6) Shake before serving. Serve cold.

Lemon Mint Liqueur

Ingredients

(for making 1 Liter, 18% alcohol)

• 460ml Vodka
• 420ml Water
• 200g Sugar
• 20g Lemon Peels
• 10g Fresh Mint Leaves

The Process

(1) In a clean, sanitized glass jar add the mint leaves, lemon peels, and vodka. Seal hermetically and store in a cool, dark place for 10 days.

(2) Once the 10 days have passed, strain the liquid from the brew into a bottle and seal. Discard the leftover mint and lemon peels or add to salad.

(3) Next, add the sugar and water into a pot and simmer while continuously stirring until the sugar is dissolved. Remove from heat and allow the mixture to cool.

(4) Once the simple syrup is cooled, add the lemon-mint extract from the bottle and stir to combine.

(5) Pour the final mixture into a clean bottle and seal for 10 days.

(6) Shake before serving. Serve cold.

Chamomile Elderberry Liqueur

Ingredients
(for making 1 Liter, 18% alcohol)

- 480ml Vodka
- 420ml Water
- 200g Sugar
- 20g Chamomile Flowers
- 20g Black Elderberries

The Process

(1) In a clean, sanitized glass jar add the chamomile and vodka. Seal hermetically and store in a cool, dark place for 10 days.

(2) Once the 10 days have passed, strain the liquid from the brew into a bottle and seal. Discard any leftover flowers.

(3) Next, add the elderberries, sugar, and water into a pot and simmer while continuously stirring until the sugar is dissolved. Remove from heat and allow the mixture to cool for an hour.

(4) Once the simple syrup is cooled, pour the simple syrup through a fine mesh strainer and add the chamomile extract from the bottle. Stir to combine.

(5) Pour the final mixture into a clean bottle and seal for 10 days.

(6) Shake before serving. Serve cold.

Veggie & Herbal Liqueurs

MIX OUR LAVENDER LIQUEUR WITH
A SWEET GLASS OF LEMONADE
FOR A DELICIOUS SUMMER TREAT.

Lavender Liqueur

Ingredients
(for making 1 Liter, 18% alcohol)

• 470ml Vodka
• 440ml Water
• 200g Sugar
• 100g Light Honey
• 100g Lavender Leaves

The Process

(1) In a clean, sanitized glass jar add the lavender leaves and vodka. Do not include the purple flowers or else it will become bitter. Seal hermetically and store in a cool, dark place for 15 days.

(2) Once the 15 days have passed, strain the liquid from the brew into a bottle and seal. Discard the leftover lavender.

(3) Next, add the honey, sugar, and water into a pot and simmer while continuously stirring until the sugar is dissolved. Do not boil the syrup, as it will affect the honey. Remove from heat and allow the mixture to cool.

(4) Once the simple syrup is cooled, add the lavender extract from the bottle and stir to combine.

(5) Pour the final mixture into a clean bottle and seal for 14 days.

(6) Shake before serving. Serve cold.

Lemongrass Liqueur

Ingredients

(for making 1 Liter, 18% alcohol)

• 460ml Vodka
• 400ml Water
• 240g Sugar
• 40g Lemongrass

The Process

(1) In a clean, sanitized glass jar add the lemongrass and boiling water. Allow to cool for an hour to extract the lemongrass flavor.

(2) Once the lemongrass water has cooled, strain off the lemongrass and add the sugar. Stir until the sugar has dissolved.

(3) Next, add the vodka and pour the final mixture into a clean bottle and seal for 10 days.

(4) Shake before serving. Serve cold.

Sage Liqueur

Ingredients
(for making 1 Liter, 18% alcohol)

- 500ml Vodka
- 460ml Water
- 170g Sugar
- 20g Sage Leaves

The Process

(1) In a clean, sanitized glass jar add the sage leaves and vodka. Seal hermetically and store in a cool, dark place for 10 days.

(2) Once the 10 days have passed, strain the liquid from the brew into a bottle and seal. Discard the leftover sage leaves.

(4) Next, add the sugar and water into a pot and simmer while continuously stirring until the sugar is dissolved. Remove from heat and allow the mixture to cool off-heat.

(4) Once the simple syrup is cooled, add the sage extract from the bottle and stir to combine.

(5) Pour the final mixture into a clean bottle and seal for 10 days.

(6) Shake before serving. Serve cold.

Indian Rose Liqueur

Ingredients
(for making 1 Liter, 18% alcohol)

- 460ml Vodka
- 480ml Water
- 120g Sugar
- 12g Indian Rose Leaves

The Process

(1) In a clean, sanitized glass jar add the rose leaves and vodka. Seal hermetically and store in a cool, dark place for 10 days.

(2) Once the 10 days have passed, strain the liquid from the brew into a bottle and seal. Discard any leftover rose leaves.

(3) Next, add the sugar and water into a pot and simmer while continuously stirring until the sugar is dissolved. Remove from heat and allow the mixture to cool.

(4) Once the simple syrup is cooled, add the rose extract from the bottle and stir to combine.

(5) Pour the final mixture into a clean bottle and seal for 10 days.

(6) Shake before serving. Serve cold.

Mint Dill Liqueur

Ingredients

(for making 1 Liter, 17% alcohol)

• 500ml Water
• 440ml Vodka
• 4ml Organic Vanilla Extract
• 130g Sugar
• 40g Fresh Dill Leaves
• 10g Dried Mint Leaves

The Process

(1) In a clean, sanitized glass jar add the dill, mint, and vodka. Store in a cool, dark place for 10 days.

(2) Once the 10 days have passed, strain the liquid from the brew into a bottle and seal. Discard any leftover leaves.

(3) Next, add the sugar and water into a pot and simmer while continuously stirring until the sugar is dissolved. Once the sugar is dissolved, add the vanilla extract. Remove from heat and allow the mixture to cool.

(4) Once the simple syrup is cooled, add the dill-mint extract from the bottle and stir to combine.

(5) Pour the final mixture into a clean bottle and seal for 10 days.

(6) Shake before serving. Serve cold.

Brussels Sprouts Liqueur

Ingredients

(for making 1 Liter, 18% alcohol)

- 460ml Vodka
- 440ml Water
- 2ml Organic Vanilla Extract
- 180g Sugar
- 300g Brussels Sprouts
- 20g Fresh Lemon Peels

The Process

(1) In a clean, metal pot add the quartered brussels sprouts, lemon peels, and water. Cook for 3 minutes on a low heat.

(2) Once the 3 minutes have passed, let the brussels sprouts water cool for 2 hours to extract the flavors.

(3) Next, strain the brussels sprouts and lemon peels and reserve the water. Add the remaining water back to the pot along with the sugar and vanilla. Stir until the sugar has dissolved, remove from heat and allow to cool.

(4) Once the simple syrup is cooled, add the vodka and stir to combine.

(5) Pour the final mixture into a clean bottle and seal for 10 days.

(6) Shake before serving. Serve cold.

Tomato Liqueur

Ingredients
(for making 1 Liter, 19% alcohol)

- 500ml Vodka
- 420ml Water
- 160g Sugar
- 200g Ripe Tomato Peels
- 60g Black Raisins

The Process

(1) In a clean, sanitized glass jar add the tomato peels, raisins, and vodka. Seal hermetically and store in a cool, dark place for 10 days.

(2) Once the 10 days have passed, strain the liquid from the brew into a bottle and seal. Discard any leftover tomato peels, but feel free to eat the raisins.

(3) Next, add the sugar and water into a pot and simmer while continuously stirring until the sugar is dissolved. Remove from heat and allow the mixture to cool.

(4) Once the simple syrup is cooled, add the tomato extract from the bottle and stir to combine.

(5) Pour the final mixture into a clean bottle and seal for 10 days.

(6) Shake before serving. Serve cold.

Carrot Liqueur

Ingredients
(for making 1 Liter, 19% alcohol)

• 480ml Vodka
• 420ml Water
• 160g Sugar
• 300g Freshly Chopped Carrots

The Process

(1) In a clean, sanitized glass jar add the carrots and vodka. Seal hermetically and store in a cool, dark place for 10 days.

(2) Once the 10 days have passed, strain the liquid from the brew into a bottle and seal. Discard any leftover carrots.

(3) Next, add the sugar and water into a pot and simmer while continuously stirring until the sugar is dissolved. Remove from heat and allow the mixture to cool.

(4) Once the simple syrup is cooled, add the carrot extract from the bottle and stir to combine.

(5) Pour the final mixture into a clean bottle and seal for 10 days.

(6) Shake before serving. Serve cold.

Artichoke Liqueur

Ingredients
(for making 1 Liter, 19% alcohol)

- 490ml Vodka
- 420ml Water
- 160g Sugar
- 600g Artichoke Hearts
- 10g Fresh Lemon Peels

The Process

(1) In a clean, sanitized glass jar add the artichoke hearts, lemon peels, and vodka. Seal hermetically and store in a cool, dark place for 10 days.

(2) Once the 10 days have passed, strain the liquid from the brew into a bottle and seal. Discard the artichoke and lemon peels.

(3) Next, add the sugar and water into a pot and simmer while continuously stirring until the sugar is dissolved. Remove from heat and let cool.

(4) Once the simple syrup is cooled, add the artichoke extract from the bottle and stir to combine.

(5) Pour the final mixture into a clean bottle and seal for 10 days.

(6) Shake before serving. Serve cold.

Kohlrabi Liqueur

Ingredients
(for making 1 Liter, 18% alcohol)

- 480ml Vodka
- 450ml Water
- 150g Sugar
- 250g Fresh Kohlrabi

The Process

(1) In a clean, sanitized glass jar add the kohlrabi and vodka. Seal hermetically and store in a cool, dark place for 10 days.

(2) Once the 10 days have passed, strain the liquid from the brew into a bottle and seal. Discard any leftover kohlrabi.

(3) Next, add the sugar and water into a pot and simmer while continuously stirring until the sugar is dissolved. Remove from heat and allow the mixture to cool.

(4) Once the simple syrup is cooled, add the kohlrabi extract from the bottle and stir to combine.

(5) Pour the final mixture into a clean bottle and seal for 10 days.

(6) Shake before serving. Serve cold.

Beet Liqueur

Ingredients

(for making 1 Liter, 19% alcohol)

- 500ml Vodka
- 50g Dark Raisins
- 200ml Water
- 40g Lemon Peels
- 220ml Beet Juice
- 240g Beets (With Skin)
- 150g Sugar

The Process

(1) In a clean, sanitized glass jar add the cleaned beets (cut into disks), raisins, lemon peels, and vodka. Seal hermetically and store in a cool, dark place for 10 days.

(2) Once the 10 days have passed, strain the liquid from the brew into a bottle and seal. Discard any leftover fruit and vegetables.

(3) Next, add the sugar and water into a pot and simmer while continuously stirring until the sugar is dissolved. Add the beet juice, remove from heat, and allow the mixture to cool.

(4) Once the simple syrup is cooled, add the beet extract from the bottle and stir to combine.

(5) Pour the final mixture into a clean bottle and seal for 10 days.

(6) Shake before serving. Serve cold.

Fennel Liqueur

Ingredients
(for making 1 Liter, 18% alcohol)

- 480ml Vodka
- 430ml Water
- 350g Fresh Fennel
- 180g Sugar

The Process

(1) In a clean, sanitized glass jar add the fennel and vodka. Seal hermetically and store in a cool, dark place for 10 days.

(2) Once the 10 days have passed, strain the liquid from the fennel extract into a bottle and seal. Discard any leftover fennel.

(3) Next, add the sugar and water into a pot and simmer while continuously stirring until the sugar is dissolved. Remove from heat and let cool.

(4) Once the simple syrup is cooled, add the fennel extract from the bottle and stir to combine.

(5) Pour the final mixture into a clean bottle and seal for 10 days.

(6) Shake before serving. Serve cold.

Homemade Vodka

Star Anise Vodka

Ingredients
(for making 700ml, 30% alcohol)

• 530ml Vodka, 40%
• 140ml Water
• 50g Sugar
• 2g Star Anise

The Process

(1) In a clean, sanitized glass jar add the star anise and vodka. Seal hermetically and store in a cool, dark place for 15 days.

(2) Once the 15 days have passed, strain the liquid from the star anise extract into a bottle and seal. Discard any leftover anise.

(3) Next, add the sugar and water into a pot and simmer while continuously stirring until the sugar is dissolved. Remove from heat and let cool.

(4) Once the simple syrup is cooled, add the anise extract from the bottle and stir to combine.

(5) Pour the final mixture into a clean bottle and seal for 14 days.

(6) Shake before serving. Serve cold.

Pineapple Vodka

Ingredients

(for making 700ml, 30% alcohol)

- 530ml Vodka
- 140ml Water
- 80g Dried Pineapple
- 55g Sugar

The Process

(1) In a clean, sanitized glass jar add the pineapple and vodka. Store in a cool, dark place for 10 days.

(2) Once the 10 days have passed, strain the liquid from the brew into a bottle and seal. Feel free to eat any leftover pineapple as an adult snack or blend it up into a pineapple smoothie.

(3) Next, add the sugar and water into a pot and simmer while continuously stirring until the sugar is dissolved. Remove from heat and let cool.

(4) Once the simple syrup is cooled, add the pineapple extract from the bottle and stir to combine.

(5) Pour the final mixture into a clean bottle and seal for seven days.

(6) Shake before serving. Serve cold.

117

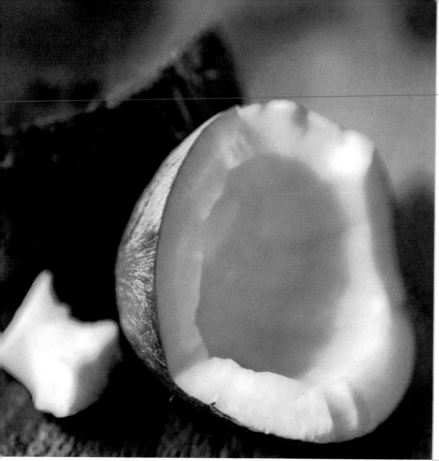

Coconut Vodka

Ingredients
(for making 700ml, 30% alcohol)

- 530ml Vodka
- 140ml Water
- 100g Coconut Chips
- 55g Sugar

The Process

(1) In a clean, sanitized glass jar add the coconut chips and vodka. Seal hermetically and store in a cool, dark place for 15 days.

(2) Once the 15 days have passed, strain the liquid from the coconut extract into a bottle and seal. Discard any leftover coconut chips.

(3) Next, add the sugar and water into a pot and simmer while continuously stirring until the sugar is dissolved. Remove from heat and let cool.

(4) Once the simple syrup is cooled, add the coconut extract from the bottle and stir to combine.

(5) Pour the final mixture into a clean bottle and seal for seven days.

(6) Shake before serving. Serve cold.

Apple Vodka

Ingredients
(for making 700ml, 30% alcohol)

- 540ml Vodka
- 130ml Water
- 60g Sugar
- 100g Dried Apples
- 40g Raisins

The Process

(1) In a clean, sanitized glass jar add the apples, raisins, and vodka. Store in a cool, dark place for 10 days.

(2) Once the 10 days have passed, strain the liquid from the brew into a bottle and seal. Feel free to eat any leftover fruit.

(3) Next, add the sugar and water into a pot and simmer while continuously stirring until the sugar is dissolved. Remove from heat and let cool.

(4) Once the simple syrup is cooled, add the apple extract from the bottle and stir to combine.

(5) Pour the final mixture into a clean bottle and seal for seven days.

(6) Shake before serving. Serve cold.

Cinnamon Vodka

Ingredients
(for making 700ml, 30% alcohol)

- 530ml Vodka
- 145ml Water
- 50g Sugar
- 10g Cinnamon Sticks

The Process

(1) In a clean, sanitized glass jar add the cinnamon sticks and vodka. Seal hermetically and store in a cool, dark place for 15 days.

(2) Once the 15 days have passed, strain the liquid from the cinnamon extract into a bottle and seal. Discard any leftover cinnamon sticks.

(3) Next, add the sugar and water into a pot and simmer while continuously stirring until the sugar is dissolved. Remove from heat and let cool.

(4) Once the simple syrup is cooled, add the cinnamon extract from the bottle and stir to combine.

(5) Pour the final mixture into a clean bottle and seal for seven days.

(6) Shake before serving. Serve cold.

Homemade Moonshine

POMEGRANATE DELIGHT, MIXED WITH A GLASS OF SANGRIA.

Pomegranate Delight

Ingredients

(for making 700ml, 50% alcohol)

- 345ml Alcohol 96%
- 30g Cinnamon Sticks
- 225ml Pomegranate Juice
- 60g Dried Apricot
- 60ml Whiskey
- 80g Dried Apple
- 80g Sugar

The Process

(1) In a clean, sanitized glass jar add the apple, apricot, cinnamon, and alcohol. Seal hermetically and store in a cool, dark place for 15 days.

(2) Once the 15 days have passed, strain the liquid from the brew into a bottle and seal. Feel free to eat the leftover fruit as an adult snack.

(3) Next, add the sugar and pomegranate juice into a pot and simmer while continuously stirring until the sugar is dissolved.

(4) Once the sugar is dissolved, remove from heat, let the mixture cool, and add the apple-apricot extract and whiskey. Stir to combine.

(5) Pour the final mixture into a clean bottle and seal for 10 days.

(6) Shake before serving. Serve cold.

Plums For Days!

Ingredients

(for making 700ml, 50% alcohol)

- 340ml Alcohol 96%
- 30g Cinnamon Sticks
- 220ml Plum Juice
- 60g Dried Apple
- 70ml Whiskey
- 80g Dried Plums
- 85g Sugar

The Process

(1) In a clean, sanitized glass jar add the apple, plums, cinnamon sticks, and alcohol. Store in a cool, dark place for 15 days.

(2) Once the 15 days have passed, strain the liquid from the brew into a bottle and seal. Feel free to eat the apple and plums as an adult snack.

(3) Next, combine the sugar and plum juice into a pot and simmer while continuously stirring until the sugar is dissolved.

(4) Once the sugar is dissolved, remove from heat and allow the mixture to cool in a refrigerator. After the plum syrup is cooled, add the plum-apple extract and whiskey and stir to combine.

(5) Pour the final mixture into a clean bottle and seal for 10 days.

(6) Shake before serving. Serve cold.

Apple Season

Ingredients
(for making 700ml, 50% alcohol)

- 350ml Alcohol 96%
- 30g Cinnamon Sticks
- 240ml Apple Juice
- 80g Dried Apricot
- 45ml Whiskey
- 100g Dried Apple
- 90g Sugar

The Process

(1) In a clean, sanitized glass jar add the apple, apricot, cinnamon sticks, and alcohol. Seal hermetically and store in a cool, dark place for 15 days.

(2) Once the 15 days have passed, strain the liquid from the brew into a bottle and seal. Feel free to eat the leftover fruit as an adult snack.

(3) Next, combine the apple juice and sugar into a pot and simmer while continuously stirring until the sugar is dissolved. Remove from heat and let cool.

(4) Once the simple syrup is cooled, add the apple-apricot extract from the bottle, as well as the whiskey, and stir to combine.

(5) Pour the final mixture into a clean bottle and seal for 10 days.

(6) Shake before serving. Serve cold.

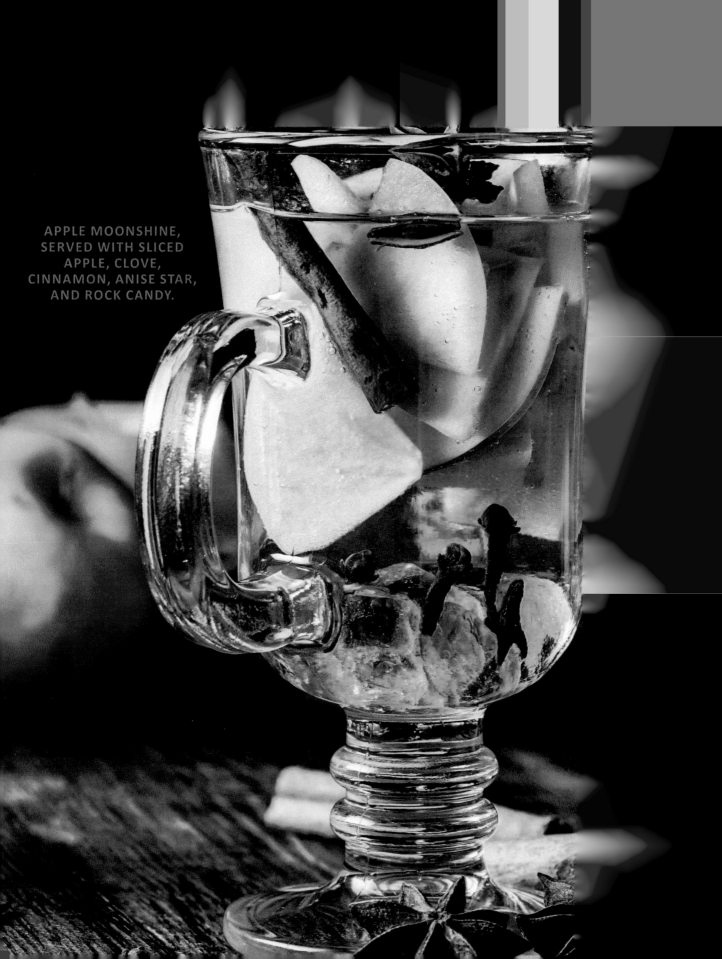

APPLE MOONSHINE,
SERVED WITH SLICED
APPLE, CLOVE,
CINNAMON, ANISE STAR,
AND ROCK CANDY.

Made in the USA
Middletown, DE
16 April 2022